Arminius or the Rise of a National Symbol in Literature

UNC | COLLEGE OF ARTS AND SCIENCES
Germanic and Slavic Languages and Literatures

From 1949 to 2004, UNC Press and the UNC Department of Germanic & Slavic Languages and Literatures published the UNC Studies in the Germanic Languages and Literatures series. Monographs, anthologies, and critical editions in the series covered an array of topics including medieval and modern literature, theater, linguistics, philology, onomastics, and the history of ideas. Through the generous support of the National Endowment for the Humanities and the Andrew W. Mellon Foundation, books in the series have been reissued in new paperback and open access digital editions. For a complete list of books visit www.uncpress.org.

Arminius or the Rise of a National Symbol in Literature
From Hutten to Grabbe

RICHARD KUEHNEMUND

UNC Studies in the Germanic Languages and Literatures
Number 8

Copyright © 1953

This work is licensed under a Creative Commons CC BY-NC-ND license. To view a copy of the license, visit http://creativecommons.org/licenses.

Suggested citation: Kuehnemund, Richard. *Arminius or the Rise of a National Symbol in Literature: From Hutten to Grabbe.* Chapel Hill: University of North Carolina Press, 1953. DOI: https://doi.org/10.5149/9781469657745_Kuehnemund

Library of Congress Cataloging-in-Publication Data
Names: Kuehnemund, Richard.
Title: Arminius or the rise of a national symbol in literature: From Hutten to Grabbe / by Richard Kuehnemund.
Other titles: University of North Carolina Studies in the Germanic Languages and Literatures ; no. 8.
Description: Chapel Hill : University of North Carolina Press, [1953] Series: University of North Carolina Studies in the Germanic Languages and Literatures.
Identifiers: LCCN 53001414 | ISBN 978-1-4696-5773-8 (pbk: alk. paper) | ISBN 978-1-4696-5774-5 (ebook)
Subjects: Arminius, Prince of the Cherusci — In literature.
Classification: LCC PD25 .N6 NO. 8

To
Julia de Kalb and Richard Lezius,
My Own.

Table of Contents

	Page
Preface	ix
Introduction	xv

Chapter

I.	From Tacitus to Humanism	1
II.	The Age of Humanism	11
	National Hero	11
	Hutten's "Arminius"	14
III.	From Humanism Towards the Thirty Years' War	19
	Heroic Nation	
IV.	Baroque Romanticism	37
	'Magnanimous' Hero	
V.	Towards a National Drama	54
	Culture-Nation—The Era of J. E. Schlegel and Klopstock	
VI.	The Struggle for National Freedom and Union	86
	Heinrich von Kleist and his Successors	

CONCLUSION: Survey of the Last Decades	105
Power-Nation and Expansion	

APPENDIX

Preface	111
Introduction	114
Chapter I	115
Chapter II	115
Chapter III	116
Chapter IV	117
Chapter V	118
Chapter VI	119
Conclusion	121

PREFACE

The purpose of this research is to evaluate the *ideological* significance of the emergence of the Arminius and Varus Battle themes in patriotic German literature. Both themes, which form but two aspects of one story, have been treated before, and almost exclusively by German scholars. But most of the earlier approaches have viewed the Arminius figure in literature from a *purely* literary standpoint. Some confine themselves to individual Arminius poets, some to special historic periods; others, again, are of a decidedly limited perspective or even obsolete today. The entire history of the poetic Arminius motif is still to be written. No English research on the fascinating topic seems to exist.

Only such poetic works on Arminius have been chosen and interpreted as seemed essential to the ideological perspective of the present study. Hence, this analysis is far from claiming completeness in the sense of literary evaluation. Moreover, what seems inferior in the light of aesthetic interpretation may often prove to be of considerable import to the social psychologist's view or to a scholarly treatment of myths and ideologies.

Thus this study is not primarily intended for the literary scholar but, rather, for the student of the emergent German national consciousness who is also interested in the more general aspects of the peculiar German national genius.

The story of Arminius actually presents itself to the modern scholar under two basic aspects, namely as a topic of factual historic inquiry *and* as one of poetic literature. Both have their roots in the same classical sources—predominantly in Velleius and Tacitus—and, after an interval of almost fourteen hundred years, both have experienced a very sudden and powerful rebirth through the antiquarian interests and patriotic zeal among the poet-scholars of the Age of Humanism.

When viewed from the historian's detached perspective, the account of Arminius' personal life and accomplishments is but part of a special phase in the general history of Rome at the height of her Mediterranean imperialism[1]. To the literary historian with a sociological bent, on the other hand, the emergence of the Arminius myth can offer fascinating insights into the soul of a nation in the making.

Therefore the following study interprets the story of the Arminius theme mainly as *Wirkungsgeschichte*. An attempt is made to trace its main ramifications and manifold contributions to patriotic thought at essential moments in German history, thus illuminating at once the origin and growth of modern German national consciousness during the course of about four centuries.

Previously[2] the theme has been dealt with chiefly in the light of *Motivgeschichte*. But it means essentially more than that. For it is also, and above all, a problem of cultural and politico-ideological history. As such its growth and metamorphosis in the course of time strikingly reflects the temper and spirit of the various epochs in Germany's tragically agitated history.

It may not be amiss to call the story of this theme a story of progressive reminiscences and of nostalgic longing; a grappling with the ultimate purport of collective living—of the life of a nation.

From the dim background of medieval chronicles, from vague memories in popular songs and distorted historical legends, the theme arises anew through the rediscovery of the 'poet' Tacitus during those youthful days of Germany's short-lived Humanism. Under the hands of Hutten and his literary successors the figure of the remote *tribal* leader gradually grows into a modern patriotic myth of *national* size and grandeur. As such he emerges from the poet-scholar's study into the bright light of every-day life and strife and soon is hailed and adopted as a cherished popular possession. He turns into a symbol of *national culture* and *Wehrhaftigkeit*—into a unifying force, a symbol of the will to national self-realization and self-defense in the ever-recurrent struggle with foreign elements and hostile forces from without.

Though not all of the countless Arminius poets have penetrated to the significant mythical core discerned in the heroic theme by Hutten, many of them do make it a vehicle for a solemn message to their people and voice through it their common fears, their hopes and aspirations. With it the poets rally the faltering parts of the postulated nation by preaching to them the courage of decision and the will to concerted action. Henceforth the *national hero* points the way toward a *heroic nation* and participates in molding his people's character and destiny.

Hence we must differentiate between the various stages in the development of this Arminius theme.

The oldest, pre-Christian stratum of which Tacitus speaks consisted of songs of praise in memory of the dead hero. These were lost during the times of migration and Christianization[3]. The next group comprises its medieval layer. While the figure of Arminius occurs neither in clerical nor in chivalrous literature, he and his great victory over the Roman Varus, in the year 9 A.D., are mentioned occasionally in medieval chronicles. Their memory re-echoes vaguely in a few popular legends and songs[4]. However, toward the end of the Middle Ages, and with a sharpened historical sense and perspective on the part of the chroniclers, the Arminius figure gradually sheds its anecdotal quality and gains again in individual distinctness.

But it was left to the humanists to turn the semi-legendary figure into a sharply delineated historical personality. Under the impact of the re-discovered classical sources—Tacitus' *Germania* and *Annals* ranking foremost among them—the regained tribal hero, though still distant, enters upon his new mission as a *historical myth,* as the bearer of a national challenge and vision by force of his superior leadership, through his character and innate qualities. He now stands out as the prototype of fortitude, of loyalty, chastity and simplicity—cardinal virtues of his race according to the Roman Tacitus. But he excels, above all, as the valiant and unconquerable *defender of his people's liberty and unity.*

For the loss of those cardinal virtues Arminius bitterly reproaches his people during the next phase of his metamorphosis as, with the internal collapse and moral deterioration in the wake of the Thirty Years' War, the *hero's mission* turns predominantly *moral and domestic.* The fantastic romancer Lohenstein, however, makes his 'magnanimous' Arminius the pivotal hero of his seventeenth-century social idealism. His baroque view and world all but denationalize the hero of this strangely quasi-patriotic *Staats- und Liebesroman.* Yet hero and author claim their nation as *die Macht der Mitte*—as Europe's pivotal power, its *Ur- und Hauptnation*. Rococo playfulness, on the other hand, soon places the strangely mellowed and shrunken figure from the tribal past upon the opera stage, while French dramatists divest the old theme altogether of its sterling mettle and degrade the grandiose struggle between nations for freedom or slavery into a plot of intrigue among unequal lovers.

But with the middle of the 18th century the Arminius physiognomy reverts once more to the truly heroic. Henceforth he lends himself to the service of the rising national stage. Here he holds high the vision of a re-Germanized national spirit by *preaching cultural integration and coöperation* among the nation's parts. With a hope for future political union, he bids his people turn their backs upon fratricidal strife and think in terms of one nation instead of petty dynasties and states. Then, in the hour of overwhelming national disaster and under the hammer-blows of the Corsican, he calls their minds away from lofty speculation and cosmopolitanism and helps turn the tide in favor of a common and dynamic *national patriotism*.

With Kleist, the greatest dramatic genius ever to avail himself successfully of the grandiose possibilities latent in the Arminius plot, we touch upon the crowning version of the Arminius theme in modern German literature. In this tragic poet himself, as in so many of his aroused generation, the breakthrough occurs from the a-political, lofty world of the abstract to the clear vision of a new citizenship based upon the ethical relation between the citizen and his political state. Though, in Kleist's case, this timely and most urgent concern did not find its highest expression in his *Hermannsschlacht* but in essays and in his unique political testament, the far superior drama *Der Prinz von Homburg*, it still was this greatest modern interpreter of the Arminius theme who did extol poetically the new political ethos. He, therefore, also ranks among the great patriotic poets, not only of his own generation, but of the ages.

What follows after Kleist in the field of Arminius literature is to be measured quantitatively rather than qualitatively, though its spreading attests to the ever-growing popularity of the patriotic theme. None of its later interpreters has altered the hero's features to any essential extent. Yet the highly gifted and personally tragic Grabbe contributed one more distinctive element by rooting his militant hero deeply in his Westphalian home soil and by pitting the rustic and morally unspoiled peasant world of the North successfully against the military might of decadent Rome in its desperate struggle for survival and national unity.

Rather death than slavery and *In unity lies strength*: these are the two major themes that run as *leitmotifs* through the entire German Arminius literature.

It seems only natural that with the progressive struggle for political union, and with its fulfillment just beyond the horizon, this literature should have reached the peak of its popularity during the course of the nineteenth century—a century of national wars, of political crises and revolutions.

Thus the Arminius literature is, by and large, *Tendenzliteratur*—propaganda, political, cultural and moral. Its theme emerges again and again in times of crises. It stems mainly from poets who are young of heart and speak to the youthful in spirit.

According to bibliographies[5] the Arminius theme has been treated poetically, and as an individual theme, about 130 times between Hutten's militant Dialogue and World War II. It is, however, most likely that innumerable versions, produced for local events on special festive occasions and by poets of little renown, have never reached the printer's press nor come to the historian's notice. Other attempts remained fragments, with some true poets among their authors.[6] Moreover, innumerable are those cases where the hero is merely mentioned, first in chronicles and later mainly in poems and songs. The 130 odd versions which are listed in our bibliographies consist mainly of dramas, operas and *Singspiele*, epics, odes and other poems. Later there appear also some prose versions which often stand half-way between fiction and historical truth.

Even a casual glance at these records reveals a constantly swelling tide through the centuries. Still the 17th century has relatively few versions to offer, though it produced Lohenstein's mammoth novel and introduced the theme to the foreign stage. Beginning with the middle of the 18th century the Arminius literature grows steadily in volume. It reaches its first peak during the Wars of Liberation and the decades after Kleist, with an ever-growing output of Arminius publications towards the end of the 19th century. After 1870, the theme mainly celebrates national greatness achieved: it looks backward rather than forward.

Our present century has added about two dozen more versions so far, with a number of Arminius novels, new adaptations of older plays, and even some radio versions, stemming mostly from the recent National Socialist era.

National hero—heroic nation—'magnanimous' hero—culture-nation and national state: those are the main steps in the symbolic metamorphosis of the poetic Arminius theme during the course of about four centuries.

The decline in the symbol's prophetic and moral force starts during the second half of the 19th century when the theme is used to celebrate the power-nation. It reaches its low during the era of national socialism when, with implied self-pride, Arminius is upheld as a symbol of the new leader-principle and of the Teutonic superrace.

* * * * * * *

I wish here to express my deep appreciation for the most generous help and interest in the process of this study on the part of my esteemed colleagues, Professors Gilbert Chinard, E. H. Harbison, Walter Silz, and Ira O. Wade, and also Professor Harold S. Jantz, of Northwestern University. Princeton University has greatly facilitated the progress of my research by liberal grants during the summers of 1949 and 1950 and has, moreover, most generously financed its publication. To Dr. John R. Arscott, of the Engl. Dept. of Princeton High School, I am indebted for his reading of the manuscript and for many helpful suggestions. The staff of Harvard's Widener Library has given me much assistance for which I am most grateful.

INTRODUCTION

Germany and the Occidental 'Oecumene'

At the outset of the Peloponnesian War Greece was again divided into bitterly competitive camps. Yet Pericles was justified in proclaiming in his great Funeral Oration, "In short, I say that as a city *we are the school of Hellas.*" Thus a great Athenian voiced not only the civic pride of his countrymen despite the turmoil of a fratricidal war: he also gave solemn expression to their common feeling of Athens' mission in Greek history.

The greatness of these memorable words lies in their marked moderation, in their long-range view and in the significant absence of imperialistic implications. The leadership of Athens was predominantly a cultural one, as Pericles and his Athenians well realized, and therein lay their hope.

The presence of such consciousness of a common historic mission on the part of a group-community, be it large or small, is indeed a healthy manifestation of an essential homogeneity beyond all inner division or ephemeral divergence. It portends unity of purpose and destiny.

Such common consciousness, however, is not an inherent group phenomenon but a historical product. Ordinarily of slow growth, it manifests itself most noticeably at moments of common stress, during dramatic crises and triumphs. It may evolve quite naturally or be fostered in an atmosphere of strife and by any kind of propaganda. It may assume political, social, religious or generally cultural aspects; or all of those at once in one sweeping assertion of predestined, innate superiority over the outside word. Of this latter, 'totalitarian' type was, among others, its recent variety in Hitler's Germany, which was at once all-exclusive and all-embracing and, therefore, fundamentally a-moral and a-social.

How such a fanatical course ever became possible among a people once as generally respected for its high level of social and cultural achievement as Germany was, is one of the many psychological problems that beset our chaotic age. No people *as* a people is, morally speaking, ever totally good or bad, though its actions and responses as a group may from time to time reflect a lower or higher level of civilized behavior. A people may even alter its group character under the impact of extraordinary conditions and unwonted experiences. Such changes have not been infrequent in history.

Yet to attribute the group conduct of nations to racial traits or propensities seems utterly unjust. A nation is a social group; and groups mainly *re*-act. Their so-called actions usually are prompted, guided or even performed for them, by a few. These few, given the opportunity and power, are always able to alter the 'natural,' i.e., expected course of historic events almost at will. The psychic relation between racial traits—a term expressing mere surface approximations—and social conduct is indeed a highly speculative proposition. Rather, the conduct of a nation may reflect the resultant of all those components which contribute to, and shape, its destiny.

The ethical progress of individuals and social groups along the thorny path of so-called 'civilization' may well be gauged by their gradual advancement in a sympathetic understanding for those who live beyond their immediate view and by their willingness to cooperate with them. Primitive man (in all ages) knows only himself, his mate and offspring. From there he proceeds to a participation in the tribal community, to village, 'polis,' and 'civitas'; thence again, as on a much higher level of individual usefulness and social merit, to the quite abstract concepts of nation and race. Only ultimately does he sometimes arrive at a sympathetic understanding of mankind at large and shape his conduct accordingly.

History records this evolution of men and groups, its high-points and low-points, on our road from *Eigenliebe* (self-love), through *Nächstenliebe* (love of one's neighbor), to *Fernstenliebe* (universal love). Actually, we live our lives predominantly within the shelter of small groups and units and feel and act accordingly. With them we share our daily fears, our hopes and aspirations; with them we feel united in a common cause and destiny.

It follows that group consciousness and the assertion of a common mission may vary considerably as to direction, purpose and intensity. At times it may be highly beneficial to its bearers and their fellow-men and be felt as such for centuries. Yet at some point it may cause stagnation or even retrogression, turning oppressive and destructive by force of its weight or intensity.

It may seem to be a peculiar social phenomenon that Germany, though one of Europe's youngest political nations, should have developed within the span of a few generations the most ardent type of a historical-mission concept. Actually, its roots go far back into history.

For more than a thousand years, Germany has been an integral part of the *Abendland,* the Occidental community. As such she has contributed her share to its spiritual growth and unity and has cherished the common Occidental tradition.

What we mean in this connection by 'Occident' and 'Western tradition' is essentially this: the nations which resulted from the entrance of the Germanic tribes upon the stage of history; a historic event of the first magnitude, for from it ensued a peculiar cultural communion and interdependence of the North, the East and the South through the blending of Teutonic, Greco-Roman and Oriental ideals, forms and institutions. For the conquering and destructive Germanic tribes at once fell heir to the dying world of Greece and Rome.

Moreover, it has been of inestimable consequence that those wandering Teutons became Christianized at the moment of their entrance upon the Greco-Roman heritage. The Oriental mind tended toward death and the beyond; the Greco-Roman, however, toward human self-fulfilment and earthly perfection. The Christian spirit, though supra-tribal and universal in claims and tendencies, is, to be sure, not of itself hostile but indifferent to earthly life. For this very reason Christianity has become the most subtle, the most spiritual and, hence, the most effective of all earthly religions. Even the naive materialism of Egypt had tended passionately towards the mysteries of death and the beyond. The pyramids bear witness to that. Christianity, however, built its fortresses beyond the clouds.

The un-Teutonic passion for death and the beyond seized the peoples of the North slowly, but it gradually filled many with a passionate zeal and ecstasy. Such leanings of the spirit were bound to bring its adherents into conflict with their Teutonic tradition and temperament, as well as with the worldly-minded spirit of antiquity. In that way, Occidental history has become the story of the fateful and unceasing clashes between those heterogeneous mental worlds. Only at rare intervals, the synthesis between them has been attained. Yet those were armistices at best. What has been termed the period of the Renaissance and Reformation in the customary sense is nothing but one catacylsmic climax of a struggle of a thousand years. Every 'Renaissance' movement strives to renew the spirit of Antiquity, its worldliness and joy of life. Conversely, every "Reformation" aims at the restoration of 'pure' Christianity with its underlying yearning for death and the beyond.

Against this broader background of the persistent struggle with the common Greco-Roman and Oriental-Christian heritage the life-cycles of the components of the Western world have run their individual course. Numerous indeed were the elements making for ideological uniformity—*in*numerable those which made for subdivision, for estrangement and diversity among its parts.

While those centralizing and decentralizing trends and forces could be kept in proper check and balance, the durability of the Occidental *Oecumene* seemed well enough assured. But where was the center strong enough to guarantee such an overwhelming, unifying force? It was Rome, and Rome alone. Located at first outside, then at the very periphery of the Teutonic world, Rome offered the symbol of religious unity, of superior culture and, in retrospection, the high standard in the art and methods of government.

For a thousand years the centralizing forces going out from Rome, or in her name, prevailed. Yet decentralizing tendencies were always there. Though checked over a period of centuries, they gradually gained in momentum and finally shattered the old, ideological unity. The break was as thorough and final as the fall of Rome twelve centuries before. What remained thereafter was chiefly a nostalgic memory: the dream of a Western European community and of a spiritual solidarity for ever lost.

But in addition to the struggle for spiritual union, Western History, from the time of the Germanic tribes to the days of

Jefferson and Franklin, is also the story of an unceasing contest between authority and liberty—a struggle for individual freedom and local independence.

The old Germanic concept of *authority* meant, above all, the duty to *protect*. It has its roots in the life of the family. Slavery in the Oriental and Greco-Roman sense was quite unknown among the ancient Germans. Aside from occasional war captives there existed but two types of unfree men: those who had lost their freedom temporarily to a creditor through unpaid debts, and those who had forfeited it for ever through felony, a crime against the community ordinarily expiated by banishment or death. Basically, the tribe was a group of free and equal people, a militant body of men in arms. Military leaders and civic officials were chosen by them and supported by voluntary gifts and contributions.

Of all the wandering tribes, the Franks proved themselves most gifted for the founding of states and for creating legal institutions. It is not accidental that the oldest document of Germanic law is the *Lex Salica*, a Salic-Frankish law code. For the Franks were the first of the wandering tribes to exchange their traditional customs on foreign soil for the Roman institutions of provincial Gaul. That was another fateful moment in Western history. Within the span of one short generation, profound innovations had come about: instead of the old Germanic system of free self-administration, there were now crown officials appointed by the king; jurisdiction in the name of a prince, instead of the old Germanic local courts of free men; administration by royal counts and emissaries enforcing royal edicts and ordinances. Conversely, the highly mixed provincial population of Gaul had long been accustomed to a sovereign-subject relationship and to personal allegiance to the emperor in Rome and his functionaries.

Those political innovations profoundly altered the traditional structure of the tribes. The state of the Franks, henceforth, consisted of the king and a group of privileged landed lords with a host of personal retinue, of tenants and serfs. Immense land grants by the ruler to his immediate followers, who in turn parcelled them off to ever smaller tenants, at once laid the foundation for the later medieval Feudal System with its highly personal lord-and-vassal relationship. Among those privileged holders of vast tracts of land, the foremost representatives of the Roman Church soon occupied the leading place. In this manner, the upper clergy easily grew into the new class of state aristocracy. The clergy soon furnished the first officials and the very pillars of the Frankish state.

Thus the developments within the Frankish domains led to another event of momentous importance: the linking of the concerns of the Church of Rome with those of the Germano-Frankish kingdom. They started its kingship on its fateful rôle in history as the Defender of the Orthodox Christian Faith—a move which found its symbolic culmination in the crowning of Charlemagne at the hands of the bishop of Rome as the first Imperator Augustus of a new and holy Imperium with universal tendencies and claims. Henceforth the Frankish kings and their later German successors knew but one major goal: Rome. Once embarked on their trans-Alpine course, they pursued a dangerously a-national Italian policy which, in the course of time, was bound to estrange the German crown from its immediate national purpose as well as from its people. Moreover, it hastened that ominous process of the secularization of the Roman Church in spirit and aims, just as it promoted the equally portentous spiritualization of the claims and functions of the German crown. Last but not least in historic importance: those trends of their early history planted in the minds of many leading Germans a firm belief in their own historical mission. From now on they viewed themselves as the standard-bearers of a new and supranational empire and their rulers as the rightful claimants to the imperial crown of the new Rome. And, as a corollary to such convictions, there must have arisen within many minds a firm trust in the other side of their mission: if their rulers were God's appointed defenders of the Faith, then they themselves were called upon to spread it among the heathens to the North and East. Crusading thus became a great spiritual stimulus for that second major phase of early German history, too: Eastward expansion and colonization, the medieval version of Germany's *Drang nach Osten*.

The profound change in spirit brought about by the process of Romanization and Christianization of the Franks in Gaul has found a striking expression in the introduction to the *Lex Salica* which dates back to the sixth century:

"The noble tribe of the Franks, *called upon by God,* brave in arms and loyal, profound in thoughts, stately in appearance and stature, *dedicated to the orthodox faith, free of heresy* - - - Praised be Christ who loves the Franks - - - For they are the people who bravely cast off the intolerable Roman yoke. It is they who upon conversion have adorned with gold the bones of those martyrs whom the Romans have burnt and cast before wild beasts - -"

In a similar spirit of stern orthodoxy, bishop Gregory of Tours went about writing his story of the Franks at the end of the same sixth century. It was to be the history of the elect people. In those two documents we encounter for the first time in Western history the concept and claims of an elect people after the Hebrew model, expressed in a spirit of intolerant self-righteousness. It was a spirit that struck its roots deeply and often bore bitter fruits for over a thousand years. It lived not only in the minds of monks and priests. It was embraced with equal zeal by many of the secular defenders and propagandists of the Faith and later found its way into many a Protestant church and heart, and in many lands.

While the Franks thus laid the foundation for the future Western European nations, the German tribes beyond the Rhine developed almost independently for about one thousand years.

The inherent weakness of the Frankish state had lain in its constant divisions and subdivisions. The weakness of the German realm lurked from the start in a spirit of antagonistic rivalry among its members and in the mixed application of hereditary and electoral principles concerning the royal succession. In the process of perpetual bargaining and unilateral concessions for the sake of their sons' election, the German kings wasted their royal powers and domains and, therewith, the unifying force of the crown. They played directly into the hands of German regionalism and promoted the further growth of local powers.

Thus at the middle of the eleventh century, while the Saxon king, Henry III, achieved complete control over the Papacy, a German archbishop, Adalbert of Bremen, the great promoter of missionary work among his northern neighbors, dreamed of a Patriarchate and a German Rome of the North. Since then, the cry 'Away from Rome' has never died down completely in German lands and, more than once, has found its advocates among highest clerical circles. The fierce struggle between Guelphs and Ghibellines, which almost wrecked the German kingship at the moment of its greatest triumph in medieval history, is but a test-case in a maze of antagonistic, domestic trends behind the brilliant façade of the imperial policy.

That the idea of empire has strengthened German national consciousness mainly in retrospect can hardly be denied. For whole centuries it had mostly retarded or even obliterated such feelings. Neither the early monastic period nor the later medieval culture, chivalrous and class-conscious as it was, could contribute essentially in this respect. The reawakening of national pride and consciousness was due largely to the rise of the bourgeoisie with its magnificent civic culture of the fourteenth and fifteenth centuries. On the whole, German regionalism prevailed for centuries while dynastic and expansive tendencies were confined mainly to high clerical and aristocratic circles.

Yet if an English contemporary of Frederick Barbarossa could ask with indignation, "Who has ordained these Germans as judges over the nations?", we may well assume that, conversely, some national pride must have swelled the hearts of Germans of all classes in view of the imperial splendor that bore their nation's name abroad. For Walther von der Vogelweide, mouthpiece and promoter of public opinion, the emperor is the one true protector of the peace and dispenser of justice, the rightful defender of Church and Faith and the leader of crusades. For Walther, Germany reaches from the Elbe river to the Rhine and, thence, to 'Ungarland.' Within its borders *Zucht, Minne und Tugend*—modesty, love and virtue—reign. Thus Germany's greatest minstrel aims to describe the confines and characteristic traits of his medieval nation and its people, while courtly poets turn again to the ancient popular motifs and sing, together with the praise of courtly *mâze*,[1] the old songs of fiercely conflicting loyalties and of the struggle between fealty and treason.

Thus the vision of a people as a national community with common interests, heroes and traditions gradually emerged. The evolution of such legends as the one of Frederick Barbarossa asleep in the Kyffhäuser mountain[2] awaiting the call to lead his people to new victories and glory, bears witness to it. But it was, above all, the turn of the humanists to Germanic antiquity and to the German past which created a new patriotism and laid the foundation for a German national character and for new national aims. It was Hutten who strove to set up Arminius as a national hero; it was the humanists who, inspired by Tacitus, first spoke again of national freedom, of German honor and virtues. They emphasized once more the German emperor's claims to leadership over all Christian nations, thus giving to the idea of empire a new national foundation which lasted through the centuries. Last but not least, Luther and some of the humanists turned to the common German tongue, which meant another basic and unifying bond among all classes of all states and creeds. Moreover, for the German language this meant a new prestige and dignity.

Beside the concept of the Roman empire there gradually appears the new concept of this varicolored federation of states as *The* German nation.[3] But even within the states that made up this nation the cultural center of gravity had steadily been shifting to the rising city bourgeoisie—a class left out politically. The great city-leagues, too, bore a decidedly particularistic physiognomy. In short, the German kingship and the German bourgeoisie had failed to become partners in politics, and the mission of the latter had remained a non-political and mainly cultural one. However, this flowering of the middle class had produced the concept of the German *culture-nation*. To this German bourgeois type the humanist scholar preached his four cardinal virtues of bravery, loyalty, simplicity, and chastity as he had recently re-discovered them in his Tacitus.

We can derive quite a clear picture of the basic patriotic views and aims of those humanists from a cursory glance at the historiography of that inquiring age when learning and intellectual achievement were the prized password to highest public influence and dignities. For Germany this meant a first experience in the democratic principle of 'opportunity according to talent'—so rare again in the centuries that followed—when gifted sons of inn-keepers and artisans could become the daily companions, preferred advisers and confidants of kings and emperors and rise to noble rank.

However, the patriotic ken and polemics of most humanists were quite limited in range. Most of them were prone to attribute nearly every excellent accomplishment in Western history to the efforts or contributions of their own Germanic ancestors.[4] Almost all of them attempted to relate the distant tribal past to the problems of their own age and were eager to rediscover the vague features of Teutonic antiquity in the character of their contemporary Germany. Men like Thomas Murner, Franciscan monk and decidedly an outsider in the eyes of the professional humanists, attacked and ridiculed their 'patriotic fancies' with little success indeed. These historians were *Aufklärer*—enlighteners in their own peculiar way. The augmentation of German glory and a just recognition of the glorious German past were their chief objectives. With the fight against the prevailing ignorance concerning their own racial background they wished to offset the reproach of German barbarism in past and present. Their main targets were 'the unpatriotic Germans at home' and 'the anti-German bias abroad.'

One could speak of two factions among those first German interpreters of their national past. The more radical ones take every opportunity to emphasize and magnify the German glory, while the others, though fewer in number, adopt a much more critical view and warn of an unscholarly bias for the sake of patriotic propaganda. But they all search diligently for the content and extent of early German history. This means a new departure from medieval views and methods and a new individual approach to their problems and sources, but also a new tendency to exploit the facts of history for moral and propagandistic reasons. For the first time the writer detaches himself from the mode of medieval annals, chronicles and genealogies which had been focused regionally upon cities, bishoprics, monasteries and dynasties. Now, and for the first time, the tendency is towards a total 'descriptive history'—a 'Germania illustrata,' a 'Germaniae descriptio' or a 'Germaniae exegesis,' as one liked to call it. It embraced geographic and ethnical features, the description of the beauty of landscape, of the natural wealth of the land and of the cultural achievements of the individual regions.

In short, an encyclopedic propensity prevailed which often leads to the display of a romantically colored polymathy.

When Enea Silvio[5] raised, for the first time, the question of the boundaries of the old and the new Germany, and when he commented at length on Tacitus' *Germania,* he gave a new and powerful stimulus to German national historiography. Now, and for the first time, German historians began to draw a line between, and compare, the 'Germania prisca' and the 'Germania recentior'—ancient and modern Germany. Some of their favorite themes now are Germany's transition from a tribal to a national state, i.e., the beginnings of a German nation and of her national history; the Christianization of Germany; the German character of Alsace since the days of Caesar; the origin of the German language; The German origin and character of Charlemagne and his contributions to German literature and culture; the universal policies of the imperial crown and the splendor of the medieval kingship which, viewed in retrospect, now kindles a new patriotic zeal. In this spirit a Sebastian Brant, a Hutten, a Wimpheling, a Celtis and Bebel regard the emperor as the long-established protector of the Faith and, hence, as the lawful head of all Christian peoples. It is his divine calling to lead the Christian nations against the Turkish danger from the East.

Likewise new is the turn to the cultural aspects of history which, naturally, leads to a spirit of keen competition between the nations and to the search for their specific individuality in past and present. In this sense, Franz Irenikus[6] speaks of the Germans as the most homogeneous and most Christian people: "Germani inter se fratres, Germani vere christianissimi." The Goths are to him the most German of all, whereas the highly critical Bebel[7] speaks of them as the Gothic barbarians.

Once Jordanus of Osnabrück[8] had expressed a common medieval view when he attributed priestly leadership (the 'sacerdotium') to the Italians, supreme temporal rule (the 'imperium') to the Germans, and foremost erudition (the 'studium') to the French. But now, each nation, and the Germans among them, claimed all those functions—at least ideally—for itself and strove to outrank the others.

Similarly Humanism, on the one hand, raises the standard of

common cultural ideals and the vision of a supra-national republic of learning while, on the other hand, it arouses a keen awareness of national individuality and, with it, the spirit of international rivalry.

In this spirit, the great Aventinus[9] emphatically rejects the assertion by the old Roman writers that German liberty had in reality been a state of anarchy. The rule of the Franks, Aventinus holds, had spelt servitude because of the adoption of the Roman church and of the Roman administrative system. But liberty had returned to Germany (i.e., East Franconia) with the advent of the Saxon kingship. While he does not mention Arminius himself, Aventinus states nevertheless that the victory over Varus had saved Germany from becoming another province of Rome. At about the same time (in 1533), Beatus Rhenanus dispelled the old legend of the Varus battle at the gates of Augsburg. He, the good disciple of Erasmus, even bewails the downfall of the Roman empire and the decline of its glorious culture. He does not see at all in the Franks the heirs of Roman culture but merely the successors to the Roman system of provincial administration. Hence he rejects the humanist's favorite theory of the transmission of the Roman empire to the Frankish state—the much-disputed 'translatio imperii' theory. Rhenanus, furthermore, ridicules Heinrich Bebel's favorite assumption that Germany is Europe's *Ur-und Hauptnation*[10]—the basic and, therefore, leading nation in European history. Rhenanus does not even grant Germany the glory of an ancient culture, as Celtis and so many others did. Nor does he see in the early Saxon kingship the natural unfolding of the German 'imperium mundi', as Celtis saw it, but merely an expedient union of German tribes. In contrast to most others, German antiquity is for this Rhenanus the a-cultural or pre-cultural period of German history whose culture developed much later, and only in the wake of her Christianization.

Erasmus and Rhenanus are about the only ones among these many humanists who realized and stressed the interrelation between peace and civilization, between religion and progress. They remained indifferent to the lures of such appealing legends as that of the Druids as a class of philosophers and 'monks' among the ancient Germans. Even the mythical descent of the

German kings and their Teutonic race from their divine founders, Thuisco and Mannus, only aroused their scorn.

Yet underneath this layer of unhistoric fancy and patriotic longing among the historic dreamers of this era there still remained the wide-spread, age-old and intense regionalism with its strong consciousness of tribal descent and local affiliation—the German *Stammesbewusstsein* which, with the passing of the great days of Humanism and the outbreak of the religious controversies and wars, asserts itself even more vigorously than before. Wholly overcome by but few of the humanists, it still is discernible even in such ardent national patriots as Celtis and Hutten, the Franconian knight. Here Erasmus, the 'good European,' forms a singular exception. In this point, too, Hutten finally had to part company with him.

However, a few basic beliefs and hopes fired the imagination of almost all these learned patriots; namely their strongly national tendencies, their firm belief in a new dawn of German culture and in Germany's just claim to leadership among the Christian nations and, finally, their firm faith in Germany as the source of true nobility. Here, too, Hutten fights among the first and foremost.

The era of the Reformation and its cataclysmic aftermath, the Thirty Years' War, brought all those anti-Roman, decentralizing and particularistic trends to a highly dramatic climax. From then on, Germany remained divided into two distinct parts: the Catholic West and South, with leanings towards the Catholic world without, and the Protestant North. The empire, henceforth, appeared to most Germans as a remote institution, outside and essentially un-German. Conversely, the true rulers of German lands now were the full-fledged *domini terrae*—the princes of practically autonomous states.

When Luther addressed himself *To the Christian Nobility of the German Nation*[11] with a comprehensive program of thorough reform for the Church, for the nation and every Christian's private life, he appealed to the emperor and not to the Church; to the lay nobility of the various states and not to their citizenry whose national hero he was to become during their short-lived hopes for a complete social and political rebirth of the nation.

But this national church was not to come about. Instead, the new churches attached themselves to the individual states, and Germany's first great national movement ended in the break-up of old political bonds.

Thus the Reformation actually suppressed once more the natural development of those social and political forces which made for national unity. During the ensuing religious wars, the promising beginnings of cultural integration and nationalization were all but wiped out. What was left of Germany after the Thirty Years' War was no longer a body of freedom-loving people, vigorous and proud, with a national vision and high hopes for their future, but a mass of despairing, submissive subjects of lordly potentates and local autocrats. Even the old concept of the German culture-nation was in complete eclipse, as it had no longer any foundation in actual facts. Therefore the literature of that period is so largely either satirical or religious.[12]

The process of a national rebirth following the Thrity Years' War could come neither from "welsch" court circles nor from the people themselves, and, hence, was painfully slow. It arose, as is usually the case in Germany, primarily from patriotic and literary circles; i.e., from the remnants of Germany's once solid middle class. The seventeenth century witnesses, beside the baroque patriotism of the Lohenstein type, the emergence of linguistic societies and learned academies. The bourgeois dislike for the 'welsch' taste and fashion among the members of Germany's baroque society, the indignation over France's high-handed and violent policies at Germany's western borders, together with the German type of 'Aufklärung' (Leibniz), all did their part. A neo-humanistic period was in the making, which strove to take up where Humanism had left off, as denominational contrasts and antagonisms faded into the background. In 1658, we hear for the first time the slogan which must have stirred many a despairing patriot, "Remember that you are a German."

For the trend of the time was toward a number of independent states and away from one unified nation. But now the 'Age of Reason' was approaching and, with the first wave of 'Enlightenment,' the time had come for the moral 'weeklies' which strove to raise new standards in the interest of aesthetic culture and moral improvement among the reading middle class. It was these periodicals—the aesthetic and moral propaganda from the pen of intellectuals—which also widened the political horizon and laid the foundation for new national interests. But the accent lay again, as heretofore, more on the cultural and moral side than on the political.

Then came the era of Frederick the Great with the meteoric rise of Prussia—the age in which J. E. Schlegel, Moeser, Wieland, Klopstock and Lessing, Goethe and Schiller were born. With this Prussian ruler a great political personality appears again on the German scene; a philosopher-king who fascinated friend and foe alike. His incredible, stoic endurance, his triumphs in the field against desperate odds, filled many Germans with envy or genuine admiration. It moved Prussia into the very center of the national scene. Thus a new national consciousness emerged, and people began to ponder once more the meaning of national pride.[13] Though this king's cultural and aesthetic tastes were quite foreign to the mass of the people, yet he set the highest standard of personal devotion to a stupendous task, of austere personal simplicity and self-denial. Soon the best German patriots of the age flocked to his standards. Even the cosmopolitan neo-humanists of yesterday now sang his praises and linked their hopes for the future of Germany to the star of this new Arminius.[14]

Goethe expressed the attitude of the young generation outside Prussia succinctly when he remarked in retrospect, "We all were ardently pro-Frederick ('fritzisch'), for what was Prusia to us?" The fires of the French Revolution, the purgatory of Napoleon and of the Wars of Liberation were still needed to arouse Germany fully and to lead or force her towards the goal of a political nation.

Schiller's inner metamorphosis reflects the distance that had yet to be covered when, in 1789 and under the first spell of the French Revolution, he remarked that patriotism, after all, was a characteristic of immature nations. But in 1804 he wrote his "Wilhelm Tell"—long after Klopstock had given his national epic to the Germans[15] and after Herder, foremost cultural philosopher of his age, had tried so long to reconcile national patriotism with the ideal of true humanity. For in his generation Herder thought he detected the qualities of spiritual leadership towards that lofty goal—the re-discovered, sacred heritage of Greece as the classicists were prone to see it. For they, too, were no political realists and lifted their human hopes above the nations and far into the clouds.[16] Their mental world, likewise, embraced both the individual and the human race; but it left out the state. Yet firmly embedded in their hearts was the concept of a nation as an almost sacred community of cultural heritage and aims.

It was left to German romanticists mainly, to open those vistas of a politically united people once more, though under the pressure of stern political events from within and without.

Thus it appears that, by force of historic experiences and memories, the political thinking of Germany has moved in forms which were either too big or too small to make for genuine integration and nationalization of her centrifugal parts. Instead, Germany developed a peculiar type of particularism with a cosmopolitan strain. National integration and political union remained the German dream of centuries.

Thence, perhaps, stems the peculiar psychic exaltation in the German's personal attitude towards his nation's destiny, which has manifested itself so often during Germany's troubled course. For the psychic content of this history has too often been engendered by tremendous inner tensions and—allowing for a few brief intervals comprising less than three quarters of a century[17]—one of its basic themes has always been the struggle for a genuine national state. It, therefore, has become a history of political frustrations and phantom dreams as Germany remained too long a Faustian Homunculus—a spirit searching for its final incarnation. Thence, perhaps, stem the disquieting features in Germany's mental physiognomy. Did not even Bismarck fail in the end to create a truly national state founded on the free consent and will of its people? Instead, his labors gave belated birth to a power-state reluctantly accepted and largely feared and distrusted at home and abroad. No, even modern Germany has never been able to become a fairly homogeneous community of uniform political will and direction. Hence the history of this 'Heartland of Europe' was destined to be turbulent and tragic.

I. FROM TACITUS TO HUMANISM

A noted Renaissance scholar[1] has called Tacitus' *Germania* the 'christening present of the ancient world to the peoples of the future.' He could have included the *Annals*, though, in either case, it took the recipients almost fourteen hundred years to appreciate and exploit the regal gift.

A distinguished classical philologist of a generation ago[2] speaks of its donor as 'the last great Roman in literature' and calls his History 'a poem in prose.' Another scholar of Roman letters[3] goes even further and asserts that 'Rome has produced but one great tragic poet and he was a historian.' Indeed, from the days of Enea Silvio, Conrad Celtis, and Hutten, when the rediscovery of his work created a sensation on both sides of the Alps, to the time of Corneille, Racine, Klopstock, Goethe, Kleist, and the present, Tacitus, the artist, has continued to exert his literary spell over the modern mind.

The key to this peculiar fascination lies in Tacitus' personality and in his dramatic views on history, on his troubled world, and on life as such, which he depicts as a great struggle of antagonistic forces, a basic contest between *ratio* (reason) and that *casus* (un-reason, chance) which modifies and vitiates life and lies at the bottom of its perplexing uncertainties. For someone who views Man's lot as an ever-repeated tragedy colored by fate, it will be quite natural to bring his dramatic views fully to bear upon his chosen heroes and events. Whether such treatment reflects upon the historian's objectivity does not concern us. We have to consider Tacitus as the poetic and political inspirer of later generations—first of the humanists and then of the historians and poets of later times. For Tacitus' legacy did become part of the ideal elements destined to shape modern nations. In the case of Germany it contributed, moreover, considerably to the treasure-store of her re-awakened national consciousness and rapidly expanding patriotic literature.

It lends a touch of peculiar irony to the picture if one recalls that the rediscovery of the long-lost Tacitean writings, like that of many others from the classical past, occurred in Germany through the stealthy vigilance and not always honorable dealings of Italian humanists who were eager to free the imprisoned ancients from the bondage of the 'Northern barbarians.'

The Tacitean Annals[4], which deal with Roman History from

the death of Augustus to the death of Nero, are also our foremost source for the personal story of Arminius up to his death. For the description of the Varus Battle, in 9 A.D., Velleius Paterculus' brief but effective report in his *Roman History*[5] must have been the most inspiring version for the German humanists. With the reappearance of the Corvey manuscript of the *Annals*, the rediscovery of Tacitus was about complete. In 1515, Pope Leo X ordered the first printing of Tacitus' *Opera Omnia*—a momentous event in history *and* literature which takes us to the very center of the age and work of Celtis, Hutten, and the incipient German Reformation.

Hence we have to deal with two major 'themes' or plots in the Arminius story, as also with two major sources. Theme I concerns the Varus Battle, which has inspired countless German presentations in all forms of literature. Theme II is the Arminius story proper: the later life and tragic end of the Cheruscan hero. This too has produced a veritable flood in German literature, and in all literary forms imaginable. Both themes have also found their way into the literatures of other lands. As to the German mode of presentation it must be emphasized that the treatment of either theme is by and large of a propagandistic nature, but now and then also of truly artistic quality. The combined plots present themselves under three aspects: 1) as a literary, i.e., artistic problem; 2) as a topic of cultural history; and 3) as an ideological problem, i.e., one of incipent national consciousness.

It is worth remembering that Velleius, an officer in the armies of Tiberius, was himself a contemporary and close acquaintance[6] of Arminius and had seen service in Germany. He wrote the brief outline of his Roman History in the year 30 A.D., about 14 years after the sudden tragic end of the conqueror of Varus. He also emphasizes the noble, extraordinary qualities of the young Cheruscan leader. Thus he corroborates the statements of our main source, Tacitus, who begins where Velleius leaves off: with the period after the fateful destruction of Varus and his legions.

Arminius, therefore, stands at the very opening of German history, and again at the moment of the birth of German national consciousness about fourteen hundred years later—an impressive figure: a hero, a liberator and unifier, as the first real 'person' and as a challenging symbol.

The Germans were fortunate, indeed, that Arminius was presented to them through the good offices of a fair Roman patriot, an eminent story-teller and an acclaimer of heroism wherever he encountered it. Without Tacitus, Arminius' belated mission, if one could so designate his rôle, would have been much more modest. But human events are shaped by ideas too, and they are the more effective if they present themselves in profoundly appealing and challenging forms. For Tacitus operates with all the resources of genuine tragedy. For one thing, he always humanizes his heroes sufficiently in order to arouse not only a maximum of interest but even a deep human sympathy or aversion. Almost every hero receives his personal antagonist—as the player demands his counter-player, his *pointeur*. At times a breath-taking tension is created, which is relaxed again by skillful moments of retardation. The hero's personal story usually plays against a background of momentous political events; often with world-wide implications, as in Arminius' case. Here, as in life and drama, personal and supra-personal elements cross each other, conflict or blend. Individual passion, intrigue and chance interfere, reshaping or wrecking great political designs while giving a sudden turn to the expected course of events. Moreover, the hero is often set off from, or contending with, the fickle mood of the masses whom he must keep under his personal spell and safeguard from the temptations of his rival. High oratory, at times with almost Homeric verbal contests, occurs. Persuasive speech is followed by counter-speech: 'X. spoke about thus,' says the writer. Thus he is able to argue both sides of an issue and to heighten tension and dramatic effect antithetically.

Tacitus' *Germania* expresses quite clearly the spirit which prompted and animated his writings, the *Annals* included. Since he realizes the terrible danger from the North, his intention is anything but to idealize the mortal foe. Tacitus is filled equally with fear and admiration. But he also is human enough to watch the enemy's weaknesses with a touch of malicious joy. For, to the good fortune of their external enemies, the gods have thrust the thorn of perpetual inner dissension, of suspicion and rivalry, into the Germans' flesh. It must be Rome's prudent strategem to foster this inner weakness if the enemy can neither be conquered in the field nor subdued peaceably. This *divide and conquer* theme is to play a paramount part in the unfolding of the Arminius 'drama.' It adds to the story its treacherous and degrading strain; and recourse to faithlessness, cunning and deceit is by no means the sole prerogative of the 'barbarian enemy.'

Unfortunately, Tacitus never copes with the basic problem *why* this Arminius turned from his double allegiance to Rome *and* his people to open revolt and violence against his former hosts. We know from Velleius that he was born as the son of a tribal leader; that he was partly reared and trained in Rome; that he received Roman citizenship, rose to equestrian rank (knighthood) and took part in Roman campaigns as an officer. Why then this apparently sudden change of heart?[7] Nowhere in the accounts of Velleius or Tacitus are we aware of a Hagen-like[8] conflict within the hero over his repudiation of one allegiance in favor of the other. We, therefore, have to assume that a better insight into the interests of his people came over Arminius upon his return home and with mental maturity. Tacitus' silence on this point could bear this out. On the other hand, the character of Varus must have had something to do with it, as the Roman sources indicate when speaking of the incipient revolt.

Velleius describes Arminius as full of youthful fire and impatient energy, and of unusual intelligence; head and shoulders above his own people.[9] Moreover, mere personal ambition could have been more amply satisfied in world-wide activities on the Roman side. Thus there seems to remain, at least for the start, nothing but an ardent patriotism as the main motive force. That is also the way posterity has viewed and adopted Arminius, at least north of the Alps.

Here we touch upon the *Leitmotif* of the entire Tacitus plot: Arminius remains invincible, as though shielded by the gods, as long as he is prompted solely by unselfish motives; as long as, to speak with Tacitus, he reflects the ancient Roman virtues. As soon as he strives selfishly after power for power's sake, he is debased and falls. Many of Tacitus' heroes, his emperor Tiberius included, begin nobly and then fall victim to that terrible temptation, the *vis dominationis*, as Tacitus terms it: a perfect case of tragedy and tragic guilt. And this holds true for his Arminius, too, if we recall the shining qualities with which both Tacitus and Velleius endow the Cheruscan initially. Does not the Suevian Marobod, temporary counter-player of Arminius in the game for regal domination, fare similarly? Only, his is not even a quick, tragic death in the prime of life. Instead he lingers on, ignominiously exiled, until he becomes a mere pawn in the hands of the Romans and is all but forgotten. "He loved living too much," as Tacitus adds contemptuously[10]; whereas the memory of Arminius lives on in songs. With the stress upon the Cheruscan's just claim to celebrity after death, Tacitus concludes his dramatic story of Arminius.

Three focal passages stand out in this account. They, above all else, must have fired the imagination of the humanists: 1) liberator haud dubie Germaniae; 2) proeliis victus (ambiguus)—bello non victus; to which Tacitus adds significantly: not in its infancy, but at the height of Rome's power did this Arminius achieve his great victory; and 3) canitur adhuc barbaras apud gentes.[11]

This final tribute was to unleash much speculation as to possible remnants of such folk literature concerning Germany's first heroic *and* historic personality. The weight of Tacitus' last statement could only be increased by his apparent regret that the memory of the Cheruscan had been unduly neglected by Roman and Greek annalists.

The Arminius story presents itself in this Tacitean version as a two-fold drama. There is 1) the grandiose political play with its abundance of dramatic moments; and 2) the family feud and final tragic end of the hero. The two are but different aspects of the same story; concentric circles, as it were, though with different radius. Tacitus always arranges his material according to locale and personalities. All major 'actors' are real characters, and he always leads towards a highly effective climax. Thus Book II of the Annals breaks off most dramatically with an almost too rapid description of Arminius' violent death at the hands of his own people.

The *basic theme of the political drama* could be stated as 'Divide and Rule' vs. 'Unite and be Free'; or, as the Germans were to see it: Roman Servitude vs. German Freedom; with the following *Main Motives*:

1) There is, above all, the long-drawn rivalry between Romans and Germans for the domination of the Rhine-Weser region.

2) Dissension in attitude towards Rome, and political rivalry among the Germans.

3) The appearance of a gifted leader who could be a bridge

of peace between the contending 'nations.' But he prefers war and German liberty to submission to Rome. He defeats her legions once and most decisively.

For the material of this part of the plot we are indebted to Velleius; for the later personal history of Arminius, we must follow Tacitus.

4) Continued campaigns with varied success do not change the basic situation: Germany is finally freed between the Rhine and Weser rivers.

5) Arminius' attempt to unify the Germans. Resentment of rival party which forms about the Suevian 'collaborator' Marobod.

6) Contest between Arminius and Marobod for hegemony in Germany. The latter is vanquished and finally flees to Italy.

7) Arminius strives for unification and sole leadership. Two possible motivations: a) to avenge himself and to attack Rome directly; b) for lust of power. The issue is not entirely clear, though Tacitus leans toward the latter, much more human, motivation.

8) New strengthening of rival party. Secret offer of Adgandestrius, Chattan leader, to have Arminius poisoned, which Rome scornfully rejects.

9) Murder of Arminius at the hands of his kin and rivals. Germany remains free but as yet ununited.

The Family Feud and Drama. The basic *Theme*: Family quarrels, personal hatred, distrust and rivalry, interfere with the political designs and hasten the hero's downfall. *Motives*:

1) The love of Arminius and Thusnelda, who has been promised in marriage to another prince; her abduction by Arminius (preceding the Varus Battle).

2) Wrath of Segestes, her father; his intrigues for personal revenge (covering years).

3) Removal of Segestes, besieged by his people, at the hands of the Romans (Germanicus); with abduction of the heroic Thusnelda and her unborn son into captivity.

4) Wrath of Arminius; his plans for revenge on Segestes and the Romans.

5) The hostile brothers, Arminius and Flavius; their dramatic meeting on banks of Weser river: foreign servitude vs. German liberty.

The personal enmity and revenge of Segestes, the father-in-law, are fused with motives of political rivalry. A similar blending of personal and political elements may be noticed in the Arminius-Marobod and other minor rivalries.

We thus observe a most discouraging picture. There is dissension within families, dissension between and within tribes and 'nations.' Rarely do human relationships and actions transcend the pale of self-interest. Outstanding exceptions are the love and unswerving devotion between Arminius and Thusnelda; the unselfish dedication of Arminius, at least in the beginning, to the cause of German unity and freedom; as also much heroic sacrifice on the part of both armies, often displayed against incredible odds and hardships.

However, for a proper judgment of the moral aspects of the story, some basic differences in concepts on the part of the two contesting national antagonists should not be overlooked. These early Germans are still firmly attached to each other by predominantly personal bonds. Their institution of leadership (*Gefolgschaft*) with its inherent concept of *Gefolgschaftstreue*—their deep-rooted loyalty to the person of the freely chosen leader—anticipates much of the inherent weakness of the later feudal system; it knows neither state nor nation. Thus their relation to the tribal community is modified by this devotion to the leader-follower principle. The private enmity between such leaders may at any time result in complete desertion of whole hosts of followers or allies, possibly with an abrupt shift in the political picture. That meant a political instability which the Romans—for whom loyalty to Rome was expected to transcend all other considerations, including personal loyalty—could but view with constant uneasiness. Much of what they regarded as moral instability and base cunning must have had its roots in these foreign conceptions and fluid inner conditions.

Yet there still remains enough of disturbing human frailty on all sides to cloud the tragic picture.

Main characters in the early part of the "drama" (Varus Battle theme) are Arminius, Segestes, and Varus. We must get a closer view of the latter two, mainly of Varus. How is he reflected in the sources?

Velleius[12] sums Varus up in a few penetrating phrases. After calling him a man "of mild character and quiet disposition"— as someone slow in mind and body whose meager energies had been sapped early in a comfortable and protracted camp-life—Velleius ends by saying: "that he was not a despiser of money (pecuniae non contemptor) was evinced by the fact that he entered his rich province of Syria a pauper and left the impoverished province as a rich man." Roman injustice, violence, greed and scorn for their German foe were to become a major theme throughout the Arminius literature, with Varus as their main symbol.

What a challenge to the anti-Roman, anti-clerical and patriotic zeal of the humanists passages like these proved to be! Here was an impelling example of heroism drawn from their own early history. But, best of all, this Varus proved to be no match for the watchful Germans under their impatient leader, though the haughty Roman viewed them as "mere beasts with human shape and speech."[13]

Segestes, on the other hand, whose name henceforth becomes a symbol of shameless treason, is Tacitus' surreptitious 'collaborator,' eager for revenge of personal insult or injury. It is he who suggests the apprehension of all tribal leaders as he warns Varus, whom Arminius has lulled into false security. Yet his efforts go unheeded. Catastrophe swiftly overtakes the easy-going Roman. "Fate guided his plans. It took the sharpness from his eyes." As though to save the Roman honor, the author adds, "he displayed more courage to die than to fight"[14]. Segestes, however, his treachery of no avail, was forced by his people to fight on their side.

Hence Velleius seems right when he assumes that Varus' character invited the revolt. He also leaves no doubt that it was the personal plan and triumph of Arminius, who succeeded despite Segestes' treachery, thus giving to the future course of German history a most decisive turn.

The peculiar similarity of this situation to conditions of their own age must have struck the humanists when they asked themselves: what might have been the course of later events *if* 1) Arminius had been vanquished, as could have happened easily, thanks to Segestes; and 2) *if* Luther's Reformation, and the rise of nationalism that went with it, had been crushed at the start? In either case, fate hung in a precarious balance. That the image of Arminius, just then rediscovered, played its part in the national aspects of the Reformation, could hardly be doubted.

Germanicus, nephew and adopted son of Tacitus' wicked

Tiberius, takes over where Varus leaves off. Anything but a Varus type, he fosters disunion among the tribes, endeavoring to defeat them piece-meal, as his half-brother, Drusus, tries after him. The characters of both appear more shadowy than does the Varus picture of Velleius. Yet they are alert and brave examples for the Roman soldiers. Hence, Germanicus appears a much abler match and counter-player to Arminius than Varus ever was. It is he who intercedes for Segestes when Segestes is besieged by his people; it is Germanicus who abducts Thusnelda and her unborn child, together with a host of Germans, into Roman custody.

We get a mere inkling of what has gone on before this German misfortune: a contest for power among the Germans themselves, between Segestes and Arminius. In this connection, Tacitus emphasizes the fact that the people leaned toward Arminius, "as they are wont to follow the bolder and more powerful man."

There is even more dissension in Segestes' immediate family: his son, Segimundus, vacillates between allegiance to Rome and loyalty to his own people.

The Segestes story actually forms a "play within a play" while repeating some of the basic Arminius-story motives. In fact, Tacitus here anticipates Shakespeare's effective device of parallels for contrast's sake. Shakespeare, too, frequently presents different characters in similar situations, while paralleling them in two families.

Segestes' main grief, however, concerns his wayward daughter, whom he must have played intentionally into Roman hands. Of this Thusnelda Tacitus says that "she had the spirit of Arminius rather than of her father." "A spirit so unsubdued" (when being captured and led away) "that from her eyes captivity forced no tears, nor a complaint from her breath. Not a motion of her hand escaped her. But fast upon her breast she held her arms, and upon her heavy womb her eyes were immovably fixed"[15]. That is Tacitus' picture of the heroine Thusnelda—worthy guardian of Arminius' child soon to be reared in captivity.

Thereafter, we are told, the Germans were divided again in their sympathies. But even Inguiomerus, aged uncle of Arminius and "a trusted friend of Rome"[16], is temporarily drawn to his nephew's side. Yet he wavers again at the next crucial moment, and for selfish reasons: "he did not wish to submit to the counsel and leadership of the younger man"—once more this motif of tragic division within the leading families, and for selfish reasons. Only Germanicus' foresight and energetic actions prevent a new revolt.

During the ensuing smaller campaigns Arminius and Flavius, the hostile brothers, meet—each trying to win the other to his side. It is one of the tensest moments of the entire plot, with speech and counter-speech, reproach and insult, across the Weser river. Though the following battle is lost for Arminius, the Romans are forced to retreat by sea and narrowly escape total destruction in a raging storm.

Then Tacitus opens a vista onto another 'play within the play': the contest between Arminius and Marobod for hegemony in Germany. It ends with the defeat and retreat of the latter. The basic issue at stake: shall Suevian or Cheruscan princes lead in a forcibly united Germany?

But therewith begins also the last Act, the Finale of a tragedy which offers a picture of human sufferings and sacrifice, of selfishness and passion, as vivid and compelling as Shakespeare ever painted.

"Marobod's royal title was hated by the tribes"[17], Tacitus asserts. For this reason some forsook him and went over to Arminius' side, thus tipping the erstwhile equal scales in the latter's favor: "sed Marobodum regis nomen invisum apud populares, *Arminium pro libertate bellantem favor habebat*"[18].

So late does this Arminius still appear as the champion of freedom. The deep-rooted inner division among the tribes is once more vividly played upon when Tacitus continues: "the Cheruscans fought for their ancient renown; the Langobards for their recent liberty; the Suevians and their king, on the contrary, were struggling for the augmentation of their monarchy"[18]. But Marobod's pride is quickly humbled into the dust.

Yet, of the circumstances surrounding Arminius' death, Tacitus speaks with unfortunate brevity. Much of them we can only guess. We hear of the hideous offer by Adgandestrius, leader of the Chattans, to have Arminius poisoned, which the Romans scornfully reject: "not by fraud or blows in the dark, but armed and in the face of the sun, the people of Rome take vengeance on their foes"[19]. Nowhere in the story does the high-minded Roman speak more proudly and nobly than on this occasion.

But of the possible, psychic tragedy within the hero, Tacitus gives but the faintest indication when he states that, after the defeat of Marobod, Arminius himself had *"aimed at royalty* and, thence, became engaged in a struggle against the liberty of his people; and, *in defense of their liberty,* his countrymen took arms against him; so that while with various fortune he contended with them, he fell by the treachery of his own kindred"[20].

One thing must puzzle the reader. On the one hand: in the eyes of Tacitus, Arminius too, dazzled by his success, finally succumbs to the Marobod temptation, lust and abuse of power. This is indeed a most tragic turn and motif—though a favorite theme with Tacitus. On the other hand, if the Cheruscans and Arminius' relatives now turn upon him in just defense of their liberty, why does Tacitus say "he fell through the *treachery* of his own kin?" Could he not be overcome in fair combat, but only by base murder? Was it treachery—or justifiable self-defense and retribution?

One is tempted to ask: Does the historian speak here or, perhaps, the tragic artist?

We must let it rest at the question. For this is how posterity has seen Arminius: as the shining hero and liberator, tragically and *un*deservedly struck down by his envious, scheming kin. Tacitus, however, sees also the other, more tragic and more human side: the 'angel' finally fallen from grace and inner greatness. That would fit much better into the view and human pattern of the tragic poet, to whom not only the humanists and poets of the future, but posterity in general, was to owe so much in tragic inspiration and human understanding. For this Tacitean Arminius is not only engaged in a gigantic conflict with the awe-inspiring might of Rome, with the dangerous particularism and narrow suspicions of his age—with a Varus, a Germanicus, a Segestes and a Marobod—but finally even with the demonic powers deep within himself.

II. THE AGE OF HUMANISM.

National Hero.

When the apostle of German Humanism, Conrad Celtis— poeta laureatus, indefatigable lover of and teller of *Amores—* gave the first lecture on Tacitus' *Germania* at Vienna University, in 1497, he opened Germany wide to the revival and popularization of Tacitus and, with it, to the growth of German patriotism and national self-consciousness.

Celtis was then thirty-eight years of age, four years older than Reuchlin and by seven years older than Erasmus. Like them dedicated to the advancement of Greek studies north of the Alps—a pioneer's undertaking in those days—he was, however, no eminent scholar himself. An intellectual stimulator, planner and promoter of learning, he typifies that other side of German Humanism—its inner restlessness and occasional instability, but also its buoyant optimism and zest for life.

These qualities he has in common with that other restless rover of his age, the humanist in knightly armor, Ulrich von Hutten. Both lavished their mental and physical resources and died well before their time. Moreover, both had been devoted friends and admirers of their humanist emperor, Maximilian, whose interest and personal efforts in the fields of the new learning and 'poetry' they strove to further and extolled. And, finally, while Hutten wrote his *Arminius*, Celtis at least planned a great patriotic epic about another heroic figure from early German history and one-time conqueror of Italy, Theodoric the Great.

We have stressed the fact that it was German Humanism, that brief Mardigras interlude of the German mind before the long Lenten season of the Luther era, which marked the turn from medieval indifference to German history to a widely advocated patriotic interest. At this point the cosmopolitan classical attitude of early Humanism becomes enlarged and modified by a new national-historic bent; an endeavor with a romantic hue, which reveals its inner kinship with the later romantic movement in Nineteenth-Century Germany. For the immediate, practical aim of the humanist generation of about 1500 was de-Romanization and nationalization of the German mind, and by way of a delving into its own distant past. As once during the earlier days of the Italian Renaissance, the longing for erudition and the *vita contemplativa* thus was stirred powerfully by that other stimulus: the urge for a *vita activa*; but this time for a *vita activa Germanica*.

Precisely at this point stands the militant figure of Ulrich von Hutten. Hutten, too, longs to be a *liberator Germaniae*; he, too, is a powerful *turbator*—an instigator of revolt[1]. Like Arminius, he receives his arms from Italy and then turns them upon Rome.

He, too, strives to unite his Germany against the overwhelming Roman might. And, in the end, he also goes down in untimely and undeserved personal defeat, having been forsaken by those nearest to his heart: by his kin, his Luther, his Erasmus; by his emperor and even by the knights.

The amazing inner kinship between Tacitus' Arminius and the German knight, who was the first to 'dramatize' the memory of Germany's first historic hero, proved fateful. Hutten, like Arminius, is at once conservative and radical. Conservative, in so far as he longs and struggles to revive the obsolete rôle of the class from which he sprang, the petty aristocracy; radical and progressive, in so far as he drives powerfully ahead toward German national consciousness and away from Italy. Yet he also wishes to see the waning imperial power restored south of the Alps. Thus, this patriot's aims are at once outmoded and modern. To them this poeta laureatus sacrificed his career as a poet and scholar. In the long-drawn struggle, Arminius becomes Hutten's day-dream—his guiding vision pointing backward and forward. In Hutten, Germany conquers Italy anew; and the dream of the future conquers the past.

A kindred spirit animates even Hutten and Tacitus themselves; namely their deep-rooted concern over the fate of their nations. Yet, whereas Tacitus is predominantly retrospective and full of foreboding anxiety, Hutten looks forward, jubilantly hopeful. Twice Rome has invaded his Germany: once with the sword, and once with the much more insidious cowl. Like his Arminius, he calls for liberation from the foreign yoke, visualizing, as he does, the dawn of a new, free age; while Tacitus calls for a rebirth in spirit and for the vigorous self-defense of ageing Rome.

Paul Joachimsen[2], in summing up the impact of Tacitus on the first centuries of modern times, draws some pointed conclusions. He observes that since the days of the founding of the science of politics by Machiavelli, Tacitus had become a handbook of the art of ruling; that the Italians interpreted him as a teacher of absolutism; the French as the representative of republicanism; for German Humanism, however, which ushered in the critical interpretation of Tacitus, it marked 1) a turning to a cultural approach to history, and 2) the strengthening of German patriotism through the study of the past ('Historische Unterbauung des deutschen Patriotismus').

Hutten signifies the climax and virtually the end of the early patriotic and dynamic side of German Humanism, if we conceive it as lasting approximately from 1470 to about 1520; Hutten's death occurring in 1523.

Ludwig Geiger[3] speaks of the three phases of this German Humanism; or better, its three aspects, as their tendencies partly blend or run concurrently. They concern, he asserts, most of all, the attitude of the individual conscience in the struggle between traditional Theology and the new learning and poetry. Phase I, Geiger holds, shows a marked conflict between the two; a decided uneasiness of conscience on the part of the individual, with frequent leanings back towards medieval Theology. Phase II, on the other hand, displays a progressive emancipation of the individual mind in this respect. The learned layman comes to the fore. Erudition and the spirit of critical inquiry are prized highly—perhaps even more highly than traditional piety. Greek gains ground beside Latin, to which Hebrew studies soon are added, thus rounding out the good humanist's sacred trinity. The practical, pedagogic side of Humanism is strengthened in the process. Princes and cities vie for the establishment of new universities and schools, for the reform of the old. A progressive emancipation from Rome goes along with it, with an ever-louder protest against Italian hostility and Italian scorn for the Gothic, i.e., 'barbarian' culture of the North. During Phase III, national concepts and patriotism grow and spread afar; polemics prevail. The inner contrast to Rome becomes even more acute. The demands for liberation from Roman universal claims, from Roman culture and encroachment, become ever more emphatic. The din of the market place permeates the quiet of the scholar's study, as the *vita activa* and the *vita contemplativa* no longer allow of a compromise: here Erasmus, there Hutten! In the end, the conservatives withdraw to the study, once for all; while the radicals forsake it and turn to the noisy market place.

Hutten's "Arminius."

Hutten is the one born politician, the dynamic political promoter and publicist, among his unpolitical fellow humanists. He wields the pen as ably as the sword and thrives on wrath, challenge and polemics. That he was a learned man who possessed high literary talent, makes him all the more effective in his patriotic zeal, for which Letter, Oration and Dialogue proved to be the natural literary weapons.

Tacitus' *Annals* were published in 1515. In the same year, in a panegyric dedicated to Archbishop Albrecht of Mainz, Hutten mentions Arminius for the first time as the 'Brutus Germanicus'—the German liberator from tyranny.

Again, in his Third Oration against Duke Ulrich of Württemberg[4], Arminius is eulogized as the savior of his country, as a shining example deserving of emulation. And a third time, in a Letter to the Elector Frederick the Wise of Saxony[5], this prince's attention is called to his illustrious 'ancestor,' Arminius, and his heroic liberation of Germany. Here Hutten not only follows closely Tacitus' final tribute to the distant hero[6]; he even ponders the question what Arminius in his nether-world would think of his descendants and country if he saw them under the shameful yoke of effeminate bishops and priests.

Here Hutten anticipates the basic thought-pattern and purpose of some later Dialogues, including his *Arminius*, which must have originated in 1520, three years before his death. It was written in Latin and, as it was merely an *indirect* attack, not translated into German by the author himself—as he did with a number of his earlier writings in order to carry his argument directly before the people. *Arminius* was not published until 1529; the Erfurt humanist, Eobanus Hessus, being its first editor.

The primary purpose of this dialogue was, of course, the glorification of the German past; and its second aim the unmasking of the Roman foe, past and present; and, with it, a powerful call to arms and plea for unity against the common foe. For, behind this gloriously conquered Varus stands a Cajetan, an Aleander, and all of their cloak and kind; as behind the old Rome stands the new, and behind this Arminius a Luther or any national 'liberator' of the future.

This little Arminius dialogue, which early editors even had excluded from Hutten's *opera omnia*, proved in the long run to be the most successful of them all. It actually marks the beginning of the broad stream of Germany's patriotic Arminius literature. Couched in the terms of a *personal* rivalry between deceased military leaders for outstanding generalship, it actually depicts a rivalry for *national* supremacy and glory. Moreover, this Arminius is to give Hutten's Germans a shining example of true manly virtues—of unselfish heroism, indefatigable and finally victorious. And, as this hero stems from their very own past, he must help them establish their place of fame in history among all civilized nations.

We have, however, to point out that Tacitus' *Annals*[7] were not Hutten's only source for his *Arminius*. Velleius' account of the Varus Battle[8] is followed quite closely. Even Suetonius, Florus and Vergil have contributed minor details.

But the immediate inspiration of Hutten was Lucian's *Discourse of the Dead*[9] of which Hutten's *Arminius* is, so to speak, a second part. There the shades of Alexander, Scipio and Hannibal had argued before Minos' court, who of them deserved the fame and title of the outstanding general in history—the Macedonian, the Roman, or his Carthaginian rival. Minos had decided in favor of Alexander; Scipio stood second, and Hannibal last.

Here Hutten begins with Arminius' complaint: he has been unjustly ignored in the contest and pleads to be heard. The three former contestants are summoned once more by Mercurius. Upon Arminius' request, Tacitus joins the court in the Cheruscan's defense. Arminius' 'Apologia,' assisted by Tacitus, who quotes at length from his *Annals*, forms the bulk of the Dialogue.

As Tacitus recites, the familiar motives of his famous account are once more brought out. However, Hutten had a *double* task to fulfill. He wished not only to establish his hero's superior generalship over his three rivals, he also strove to remove *any* suspicion of selfish designs and of treason against his own people from Arminius, which Tacitus had implied. For, only an absolutely faultless hero could serve Hutten's patriotic purpose. Any fickleness, even the temptation of selfishness, had therefore to be removed. With that, the elements of *inner* drama and psychic conflict also had to be abandoned.

Here, then, lies the basic difference between Tacitus and Hutten: Tacitus wants human drama, while Hutten has to drive at absolute human greatness.

Nevertheless, the basic points and pattern of Tacitus' report still are clearly discernible. Arminius proceeds directly from Tacitus' testimony and its high-points: 'liberator haud dubie Germaniae'; and 'proeliis victus—bello non victus'. What has he himself to add in the defense of his claim?

The following points and motives evolve in the further course of the dialogue:

1) Arminius was young and quite inexperienced—a most welcome trait for Hutten, no doubt: An Achilles or Siegfried figure![10]

2) Arminius points out (as Tacitus had done before him) that he, the Cheruscan, had challenged the Romans at the very peak of their power; thus—the greater the glory.

3) Never has there been a larger and mightier empire in history than the Roman was, but he (Arminius) was the only adversary of Rome who was *not* defeated by her in the end[11].

4) Arminius then asserts most emphatically that he *never* had striven for personal gain or glory, but *for the liberty of his people alone*—virtue being its own reward. (This, then, in contradiction to Tacitus.)

5) Arminius maintains that none of his rivals, not even Hannibal, had first to overcome such desperate adversities at home: his country thoroughly weakened by the enemy and torn in factions—he had nothing but his youth, his resourcefulness and courage to draw on. Once having challenged the foe, he first had to create and discipline an army—and this not only under the eyes of a suspicious enemy, but even in the face of extreme want and poverty, and with no support from without. Even the enemy's (Varus') haughty disdain for him and his weakness he had contrived to turn to strategic advantage through relentless surprise actions. The salvation of Germany lay in his hands, and in his alone! (Here Velleius and Tacitus concur.)

6) After having established proof of his own ingenious generalship, Hutten's hero touches but briefly upon the tragic, *personal* side of his gigantic struggle: the paralyzing inner division and political rivalry, even within his own family, which Tacitus had described at considerable length. For Tacitus is primarily interested in the human aspects of history—in people and their fate. He ponders life and judges men. Hutten's Arminius, however, barely mentions Segestes' abysmal treachery and the sufferings of Thusnelda; whereas Tacitus tells the whole story. But concerning the repeated plots against Arminius' own life, Hutten deviates completely from his Roman source by putting those assassins into the employ of Rome. (Tacitus, conversely, reported only the case of Adgandestrius and his sharp rebuke by the Romans!)

7) The moral resurgence of Germany after the defeat of Varus, which Hutten's Arminius claims as his greatest achievement: traitors, collaborators and payers of tribute to Rome "who are no Germans" were punished or driven out. (Thus Hutten turns Tacitus' motif of continued political agitation and military reorganization on Arminius' part into a *moral* mission.)

8) The rivalry and defeat of Marobod, king of the Suevians, who strives for regal power. (In concurrence with Tacitus' account.) This is related by Arminius as final proof of his unselfish, patriotic intentions; as also of the utter injustice of his untimely and shameful end. True virtue, he exclaims, is for ever the preferred target of human baseness—of envy, suspicion, and wilful misrepresentation.

Thus Tacitus furnished Hutten with his highly dramatic material. However, the motif of the 'fallen angel'—the hero who succumbs in the end to the temptations of power—Hutten was forced to turn into the motif of a righteous St. George with the flaming sword. In order to achieve this metamorphosis, Hutten had to refute the reproach of treason against Rome, too; for Arminius had served her as an officer. The last third of Hutten's Dialogue serves precisely this purpose.

Minos declares himself convinced of the justice of Arminius' claim. He even adds that he well remembers his surprise at finding so much heroism at that time even among the barbarians: "-equidem memini admiratum tunc, istusmodi ferre industriam barbaricam"[12]. Speaking of Arminius directly, Minos even adds, "minimumque vitiis concesserit". But that can only mean: 'nor has he (Arminius) allowed evil to get power over him'; or, even more directly: 'You stand absolved, for *you have withstood* the temptations of power.' That was the Arminius Hutten needed! For he does deserve the title of the most free, most invincible, and most German of them all: "Cheruscus liberrimus, invictissimus et Germanissimus"[13].

Alexander's objection because of the hero's one-time 'servitude' to Rome, Arminius proudly rejects with a claim to his freedom in spirit at all times. Here Hutten rises to true heights of warmth and noble fervor: the reproach of treason to Rome, Arminius refutes by asserting that no tyranny ever deserves or warrants abiding loyalty; that rising against it at the propitious moment is a free man's right, duty and glory. For, no rightful claim has he, Arminius asserts, who 'robs men of nature's great blessing, liberty': *"nam quod jus habere potest qui naturae beneficium alteri eripit?"*

Thus speaks Arminius-Hutten to his countrymen; and, indeed, not only as an ardent patriot but also as a surprisingly enlightened man whose vision seems ahead of his time by centuries: tyranny, justice and loyalty are forever incompatible. No man giving his pledge in good faith will endure future slavery. Hence, revolt against tyranny, against power abused, can never be treason!

Thus Varus stands here for the entire Roman system, past and present, for inhuman encroachment upon man's natural right to freedom. The shining figure of this 'Brutus Germanicus,' however, stands for the timeless outcry against oppressors of all ages: *"In Tyrannos!"*

That, for Hutten, is to be the legacy of his hero; the message of his new Brutus.

Thus it was Hutten, the knight and the humanist, who, by exploiting his Tacitus freely, gave to the incipient German national consciousness a most powerful impetus and to its patriotic literature one of its most cherished themes and idols: a champion and a symbol of German unity and liberty.

In this unique *Arminius* Dialogue the militant, national side of German Humanism reached its peak.

III. FROM HUMANISM TOWARDS THE THIRTY YEARS' WAR.

Heroic Nation.

We have observed that the obvious indifference of most medieval German historians towards Germanic antiquity was followed by a considerable amount of patriotic interest on the part of the later humanists. Yet they, at the start, seem prompted more by a philological and generally antiquarian curiosity than by actual patriotic ardor. Nevertheless—and especially under the impact of the far-flung 'Germania' debate—that change did occur, and Hutten signified the climax of the new patriotism turned militant. The later 16th Century even "Germanized" Arminius' name and as 'Arminius' *or* 'Hermann,' the Cheruscan now joins the ranks of other popular heroes from the German past—some recently re-discovered. Thereafter he frequently is linked to them in literature. But time and again it is this Arminius or 'Hermann' who out-ranks them all as an example of *personal heroism* and a symbol of the heroic struggle for national unity and freedom.

Still, it is indicative of the slowness in the de-Romanizing process of the German humanist's mind that even such an ardent patriot as the learned pedagogue Jacob *Whimpheling*[1], could say of Varus' destruction at the hands of Arminius: "Varus de Germanis *rebellantibus* deletus est"—he perished at the hands of the *rebellious* Germans. For some time yet, the Roman-trained German humanist refers to his Teutonic forbears as 'barbari'—much as he detests that term in the mouth of his Italian contemporaries.

In 1470, Tacitus' 'Germania' was printed for the first time, in Venice. In 1477, Johann *Nauclerus* came to the newly founded University at Tuebingen in order to train young men in the study of ancient German history. This decade saw a new beginning of scholarly interest and investigation of the German past. Celtis' lectures on Tacitus' 'Germania' at Vienna, in 1497—under the specific auspices of his humanist emperor and friend—marked a first climax for the national endeavor of the new learning.

Yet, this promising new turn of the German mind was to last for only 50 short years, when Humanism was replaced—at least in weight and popular appeal—by the much more active and militant spirit of the Luther era. On the other hand, Hutten's 'Arminius' was by no means his only tribute to the national aspects of the new religious movement. Beside his massive support of Luther through a series of flaming Dialogues, it was Hutten who had signalised the momentous turn from Latin to German, thus raising the popular tongue to vie with the tongue of the learned—as Dante once had done in Italy. In this respect Hutten is the most powerful ally of the great religious reformer.

Yet there remained a deep-rooted difference in spirit between the leanings of the humanists and those of the religious innovators. It is not accidental that so few of the humanists actually broke with the old creed. More contemplative than active by temperament—more reluctant and critical than militant and radical in their attitude towards the concerns of the day, most of them rejected the final break with Rome. Their minds had become too much secularised; their bent was above all philologic-historic and critical—and not theological. Erasmus, the greatest of them, bears that out. They did not wish to become absorbed again in staid dogmatics as they sought new fields to conquer, new points of view to test.

Once these humanists had colored their histories with national propaganda. Now the Lutherans quickly adopted Arminius as a symbol of their partisan cause. Was the Cheruscan not a "protestant" at heart?!— The search for national heroes had long been a favorite pursuit; now one began to test their worth from a factional and far more practical point of view; while, under the weight of circumstance, the old vision of national union gave way once more to a new type of inner division.

A new particularism was indeed in the making. Already Hutten had fought it quite desperately. He viewed with alarm the steady advancement of the petty German princes (the independent future states) at the expense of the imperial power; just as he witnessed the crown's waning hold on Italy. It was Hutten, in the lead of the humanists, who urged the Turkish war; who strove to strengthen the crown and pit the weight of the cities, of the united knights and peasants, against the decentralizing tendencies within the realm. For this purpose, too, Arminius and the glory of the German past had been conjured up by the humanists.

What Hutten could not foresee was that the new state-churches would lend an additional power and spiritual halo to the already advancing independence of the new "domini terrae", thus furthering decentralization far beyond the dividing line of the creeds.

Hutten's last days must have been bitter, indeed, when—in addition to his personal defeat—he had to witness the death of the German, Maximilian, and Charles V.'s accession to the German throne.

It is interesting to note that a monograph, the first German treatment of Arminius during the days of the well-advanced Reformation, originated in 1535 in the land of the Elector Frederick the Wise of Saxony (+1525). It came from the pen of his former private chaplain, chancellor and most trusted adviser, who felt so warmly and had worked so valiantly for Luther's cause: Georg *Spalatin*. When we consider that it had been the good German patriot, Frederick the Wise—once a potential rival of the Spaniard Charles for the imperial throne—who, under the influence of Hutten and Spalatin, had shielded Luther at Worms and thus had saved the Reformation and the Luther Bible, the Luther-Hutten-Arminius relation moves into an interesting perspective.

Already in 1532, Johannes *Cario* had mentioned Arminius in his *Chronica*. Many other chronicles of that time do so, but Cario was the first to do it in German. His work was published in Luther's Wittenberg.

At about that time, the great humanist Johannes Aventinus[2]—'father of German historiography,' pupil and friend of Celtis and official Bavarian historiographer—briefly sings Arminius' praise in his *Bavarian Chronicle*, a popularized German version of his Latin *Annals*.

In 1535, George *Spalatin's* German Arminius monograph was published, and likewise in Wittenberg.

The confessional forces were about to clash and the political side of German Protestantism had long since proved its inner weakness: the split between Switzerland and Wittenberg seemed irremediable. However, the days of Protestant Union and Catholic League were not yet at hand. Only the frequent absences of the Catholic emperor from Germany granted the hard-pressed Lutherans delays and temporary succor. But now it was their freely chosen emperor who employed the deceiving tactics of 'divide and conquer.' At Mühlberg, in 1547, he struck the Protestants a crushing blow. Luther had died the year before. As the victor of Mühlberg, in armor and on horseback, Charles V. had his famous picture painted by Titian. The Lutheran cause was at its lowest ebb; its heart needed courage and comfort indeed.

The title of Spalatin's work is enlightening in this respect: *"Of the beloved* ("teuer") *German Prince, Arminius"*[3]; with the sub-title, "A brief excerpt from trustworthy Latin sources, compiled and translated by Georg Spalatin."

This Georg Spalatin—humanist clergyman, biographer, translater and historian, skilled diplomat and chief organizer of the new state-church of Saxony, was in many ways an unusual man. The trusted friend of leading Catholics and Protestants alike, he was a person of widest connections and weight among princes, clergy and scholars. His voluminous correspondence has become a source-book for the history of the Reformation era[4]. It is characteristic of the man's steady character that he promptly rejected Hutten's radical political schemes. It was Spalatin who advised his prince at the momentous election of Charles V. at Frankfort; it was he who attended Frederick the Wise at the emperor's coronation and who directed his sovereign at Worms concerning Luther. It was he, once more, who, at the Diet of Speyer, in 1526, deeply impressed the princes and large masses of the people with his powerful outdoor sermons on the Protestant creed.

Thus, Spalatin's Arminius treatment stems from the very heart of the Protestant movement. "May God grant that we Germans become German again," he once wrote when discussing Luther's burning of the papal bull. His Arminius essay similarly reflects the patriotism of this tolerant yet dynamic man. It is not a historical novelty but, rather, a playful exercise in warm patriotic expression while it also reflects the writer's enthusiasm for Tacitus, aroused on the occasion of a visit to the Teutoburg Forest, locale of the decisive Varus battle.

The work was dedicated to the new ruler of Saxony, Johann Friedrich, who cherished Spalatin as much as his predecessor had ever done. The monograph was soon translated into Latin for use in learned circles.[5] Both Latin and German sources were used by Spalatin. The entire story of Arminius is told, up to his death, in 33 chapters.

Riffert[6] briefly analyses the monograph and stresses as the author's aim "not so much historical accuracy as the edification of the reader"; preferably the Protestant, no doubt. Actually, the little work stands halfway between fiction and truth. Poetical license is used freely; and not only as to localities and names, but even as to facts. Yet it is a pious, upright attempt; 'propaganda' in its best sense, characteristic of a time full of fear and doubt to which it preaches integrity and courage. Its most interesting feature, however, is the fact that here, for the first time, Segestes—Tacitus' and Hutten's traitor—becomes an honest, upright man who acts in good faith in trying to conciliate the warring parties: high proof of Spalatin's own conciliatory attitude towards the contesting creeds.

But from now on, Arminius under the spell of Spalatin remains the "teurer Held," the beloved hero—the pride of his people in times of good fortune, refuge and rallying point in times of distress.[7] Henceforth, the events of the remote German past are related again and again to the issues of the present as the authors warn, chide, plead and promise. This tendency becomes even more pronounced as we draw nearer in time to that cataclysmic aftermath of the religion contest, the Thirty Years' War.

There still is extant a touching folk poem of 18 stanzas, from the year 1548, which reveals the now popular trend of the Arminius theme, just 28 years after Hutten's Latin dialogue. It dates from the distressing period after the Mühlberg battle and bears the title: "Klag und Bitt eines sächsischen Mägdleins"[8] (lament and prayer of a Saxon maiden). Here the girl laments the loss of German stamina, unity and freedom, and prays for deliverance from the foreign yoke (Charles V.). Here foreign tyranny is no longer Roman alone but Spanish—though in alliance with popish deceit. Again the vision of Arminius is linked with others, in this case with Emperor Otto III. They are conjured up for new hope.

The last stanza of the poem is a promise to God to abide by his will and a prayer for deliverance from Pope and Spaniard:
Lass uns bleiben bei Deinem Wort,
Steure des Papstes und der Spanier Mord[9].

The first of the above two lines links the poem directly with that famous Luther hymn to the tune of which it is to be (and doubtless often has been) sung: "Erhalt' uns, Herr, bei Deinem Wort," once intoned by the defeated Protestant troops on the evening after the Mühlberg battle.

Thus, hardly three decades after Hutten's militant dialogue in Latin, the hero's vision is conjured up in a popular song; his praise is sung to the melody of a Luther hymn: the soldier of God and the political liberator of a distant past have now joined hands, as patriotic folk song and Protestant church hymn blend.

In another, quite lengthy poem of the year 1546, by one Johannes *Schradin*[10], Arminius and Emperor Frederick Barbarossa, in the strange company of the soldier Frundsberg, appear to the poet in his dream. They inquire about present conditions in Germany and rebuke the present generation. Arminius angrily counsels the Protestants:
Far better were it to die at once,
Than to rot in disgrace day after day—

Again the Cheruscan and the glorious past are conjured up in order to strengthen the will of resistance among a generation so shamefully lacking in the qualities of their ancient heroes.

The theme of a poet's vision of the heroes from a better past is taken up again about one century later and on a much broader and more elaborate scale, in Hanns Michael *Moscherosch's* prose story, *"Gesichte Philanders von Sittewald,"* which originated during the last phase of the Thirty Years' War and was published two years after the war's conclusion.

But before turning to Moscherosch, one more poetic approach to the Arminius theme from the later part of the 16th century may be noted.

It is a school comedy in classical Latin in which Arminius appears for the first time in a minor and, indeed, a somewhat amusing rôle, namely that of a traveler's guide; and this time not to the past but to 16th Century Germany.

The author is Nicodemus *Frischlin,* Latin poet and philologist, good Protestant and patriot. Frischlin was a gifted but restless man, a wandering post-humanist and forerunner of the Baroque, versifier of classics and of history.

In his best comedy, "Julius Caesar Redivivus" (1584), Caesar and Cicero come to life again—though this time not in a dream vision—and set out on a northern journey. The Erfurt humanist, Eobanus Hessus, is Cicero's well-chosen traveling companion, while Caesar is accompanied—and equally fittingly—by the great warrior, Arminius: erudition and heroism journey together and admire the cultural accomplishments of modern Germany. Mercurius is the guide of the shades from the nether-world and introduces the play—doubtless a reminiscence of Hutten's dialogue—while Pluto concludes it. But behind this Eobanus Hessus stands Frischlin himself, as behind Caesar stands the modern German emperor. The play is steeped in patriotic polemics and thus assured of a generous appeal to its agitated age.

Thus Arminius has actually invaded the stage, though in a secondary rôle and in polished Latin. Later, Jakob Ayrer, Hans Sachs' pupil and dramatic rival, translated him back into his German tongue.

The play has a strong element of social satire which reminds one of Murner and Sebastian Brant. It abounds in Aristophanic humor and wit, though its structure is rather loose and weak.

The learned, fearless *Moscherosch* (1601-'69) reflects most strikingly the conflicting elements of his troubled times: the political with their patriotic impetus; and the cultural with their cosmopolitan and standardizing tendencies which followed, above all, the French cultural pattern. The former as the more popular ones are, by nature, more aggressive and self-assertive; the latter, confined as they are to 'social' circles, are on the whole imitative and, to a certain degree, self-effacing.

Spain, Austria and Bavaria had long become the leaders in the Counter-Reformation, now steadily advancing, with Catholic France as the political antagonist and shrewd counter-player to the mighty Hapsburgs and their satellites. Her political intrigues reached far into protestant Germany, into Hesse and Saxony and over into Lutheran Sweden, thus making her cultural leadership still more attractive to the Protestant princelings of Germany.

After its first bewilderment over the scope and impact of the Lutheran revolt, Catholicism itself had quietly undergone its own reform in spirit. Inquisition, Index and Jesuitism had shown their strength and had pushed the forces of the Reformation into the political defensive. Catholicism's immense inner discipline, with its complete subjugation of the individual will to the demands of spiritual authority, had proved more than a match for Luther's unpolitical gospel of the 'Freedom of a Christian.' Since 1608-09, Protestant Union and Catholic League were facing each other, with the political antagonism of France and Spain looming in the background. However, from the Thirty Years' War, which began as a religious contest and soon deteriorated into a political struggle, only one group emerged victorious: the territorial Princes of Germany—well trained, well armed and politically all but independent. Therewith, particularism had actually triumphed. The former 'Bundesstaat' (federal state) had changed into a shadowy 'Staatenbund' (a loose confederation of states) whose members followed freely their individual foreign bents, politically as well as culturally.

Thus Moscherosch was not only born into a state of political and cultural decline, which included the once great German civic culture, but also into an era of the advancing internationalization of social culture. Yet, while England and France had been able to integrate their best national forces, Germany had become the battleground of Europe for almost a century. The Thirty Years' War merely marks the climax of her political disintegration, followed by a breakdown of her entire economic, social and moral order. While France was thus placed in the social and cultural lead on the continent, it was only natural that prostrate Germany should look for guidance from her more fortunate Western neighbor.

Yet it would be quite wrong to speak of an extinction of German national feeling during those decades of trials and sufferings. Quite the contrary is true: hand in hand with the appalling moral decline, with the brutalization and political apathy of the masses in the wake of the calamitous war, goes a marked intensification of the patriotic and moral fervor among learned and literary circles. Moscherosch is but one example. The foundation and activities of the far-flung Seventeenth Century 'Sprachgesellschaften' (literary societies) bear witness to it.

Moreover, a general moral and cultural decline is discernible long before the war. The inspiring enthusiasm of the Reformation period had soon died away under the sterilizing crust of dogmatic quibbling and intolerance. The spirit of ascetic ardor and moral elevation among the masses had been replaced by a new wave of coarse sensualism, while the new religious division was accompanied by a new hatred and suspicion of one's fellow men of the opposite creed. Last but not least, another progressive inner division made itself felt more and more acutely: here the prince, his court and his French-inspired nobility—there the masses of docile subjects, the 'plebs' or 'canaille,' bourgeois and peasant alike. A spirit of abject submissiveness had replaced the promising spirit of individual freedom and initiative which Humanism and the early Reformation had bred and fostered. To the pressure from without was now added an increased pressure from within.

Viewed in this light, the strongly foreign (mainly French) cultural leanings of so many German courts and nobles (despite some remarkable and highly encouraging exceptions)—this undignified and indiscriminate imitation of foreign ways at the expense of their own national culture and tradition—could only mean one thing, namely a calamitous setback for the cultural and moral rehabilitation of the people; an additional insurmountable barrier between them and their leaders. Thus, the German voice that once had cried out against Roman arrogance, against popish power and encroachment, now turned westward—but this time in bitter self-reproach. No longer is everything German categorically deemed as good as (or even better than) everything foreign. Not that one protested against sound cultural contact and exchange, against ideal stimuli from abroad which had always existed. Even now, the young German nobleman received his best training at foreign courts, while the typical Seventeenth Century wanderlust lured German students abroad to many a university in many lands. No: here, and for the first time, the German accuses himself before the heritage of his own past. He stands accused of de-Germanizing and destroying his own national spirit; of making himself the butt of foreign contempt for such undignified bearing.

That is the basic meaning of Moscherosch's fantastic *"Visions of Philander of Sittewald"*[11].

This Moscherosch, however, is neither chauvinist nor national fanatic. On the contrary: he, the cultured gentleman, was personally quite tolerant in his religious and political views and even an admirer of Louis XIV. and his Paris. But when the interests of his nation are at stake, then the ardent patriot asserts himself as a pleading moralist who preaches, like his forerunners of the late 15th and early 16th centuries, by means of biting irony, satire and merciless self-exposure. In order to drive his point home with the masses, he often is brutally frank. Thus he becomes on occasion as plain and coarse as they are. Then his contempt of 'welsch' comprises everything un-German, everything borrowed from the 'Romance' cultures—be it Italian, Spanish or French. It aims at speech, at fashion, at manners or mode of thought; for they are *'à la mode'* ('alamodisch'), i.e., unnatural for a German and therefore, to him, frivolous and contemptible. Admirable though some of those features may be in themselves or in their own setting: a true German apes no one! That was a courageous criticism of his own age.

Yet, while Moscherosch appears most sound and tolerant in many ways, he seems in others surprisingly narrow to his modern reader. On the one hand, this German of Portuguese descent saw the princelings and their retinues squander their people's meager means recklessly and in a senseless imitation of foreign 'absolutism,' elegance and style; on the other hand, he beheld the desperate want of the suffering, mute German masses. Yet, in spite of Moscherosch's avowed admission that many things German have become quite bad of late; that many things foreign are truly excellent and that in some ways his Germany is soundly indebted to her Romance neighbors, his book still contains elements which lend themselves to chauvinistic exploitation.

However, we owe it to the poet to appraise him in the light of his own age. What he perceived about him was also a steadily mounting foreign influence upon all sides of German social and mental life; and this at a time of Germany's utter helplessness and exhaustion. Therefore the author rises in wrathful protest and points the way back to the old-fashioned, substantial German simplicity, integrity, modesty, and loyalty to the national tradition. Like the best of his contemporaries, he aims at a spiritual re-birth and at the unity of his tragically torn nation.

The visions from the past are called upon to chastise and arouse a generation so unworthy of their heroes' deeds and memory. Thus here, too, Arminius appears as the moral warner, though in a very minor rôle and in a group with others. In fact, here Arminius merely 'is there.' By his mere presence, he reflects an ideal state of manly virtues and opposes the ruinous political apathy of this new un-German generation.

How much he merely represents a type is evinced by the fact that, in the lengthy trial of Philander, he speaks but twice and quite briefly. Stripped of all traces of genuine individuality (as are the other members of this phantom court) he stands there statue-like as one in a group; and not even as the leading figure. For, in this the 'duke' is outranked by the king, Ariovistus, as the presiding judge; even by Ariovistus' mouthpiece, Thurnmeyer[12], who writes the opinion and pronounces the sentence at the end of Philander's exhausting trial.

What happens is briefly this[13]: Philander of Sittewald, with a Greek first name and a family name which suggests moral regeneration, has fallen under the sway of an imaginary court of shadows from the past who bid him answer and atone for the sins of his generation: Philander represents his hapless, wayward nation.

The court is composed of a group of worthy stalwarts from the remote past, one mythical (Saro), three historical (Arminius, Ariovistus and Widukint), augmented by some minor figures from Caesar's writings. Unmitigated enmity for Rome and disgust with the present-day Germans are their common characteristics.

By this merciless phantom court Philander is 'taken apart,' until there is nothing German left of him but a miserable wretch of foreign hue and color: his dress, his food, his speech, his courtesies and manners are all preposterously 'welsch.' In fact, he has nothing to prove his national origin and character but the pathetic story of his miserable sufferings and poverty hiding behind a gay, foreign façade, all of which, in the eyes of this court, he has brought on himself. And his sentence is this: he is not allowed to leave the precincts of the court without permission; at least not until he pledges most solemnly 1) to re-Germanize himself and 2)—and most of all—to re-educate his fellow Germans in the truly German ways. Ariovistus expressly demands a return to the four cardinal German virtues of bravery (or fortitude of heart: 'Tapferkeit'), manliness, sincerity and loyalty.

The scene is the castle of Geroldseck. Here, according to a legend which parallels the more famous Kyffhäuser saga, these visions from mythology and history appear, whenever Germany is threatened with destruction, in order to offer her imperiled people comfort and counsel.

But even this presiding, royal Ariovistus has never been able to forget that Caesar once referred to him as a German boor ('tölpischer Deutscher'). Thus, even he is to share in the German sensitiveness to foreign slight and criticism which so often in history has betokened a deep-rooted feeling of political and cultural inferiority. It asserts itself historically first towards Rome and Italy, then towards France and Spain, and finally even with reference to kindred Britain. Much of the patriotic literature of Germany seems to have its roots in this peculiar psychic condition. It certainly permeates Moscherosch's *'Philander of Sittewald'*. For with Moscherosch, too, 'Roman' still stands primarily for treacherous and tyrannical; as *'welsch'* means frivolous insincerity and effeminacy; true German, however, signifies those cardinal virtues of freedom, simplicity, sincerity and loyalty.

Yet, on the whole, these cloudy elements appear, in Moscherosch's case, more than outweighed by tones of genuine social and moral concern. "Woe to the servant," we are told, "who becomes disloyal and a traitor to his master or his country; how dare his children harbor hope of future welfare? And woe onto the sovereign and master who disposes of a servant because he can not be but frank and sincere." Thus Moscherosch pleads against the bigotry and fawning servility so common in his age. "Effeminatissima virorum pectora," Widukint cries out over the present, unmanly generation; while Ariovistus has a passage quoted from Aventinus[14] where Charlemagne chides his Franks who adopt the 'French' style: "You conquer nations and are conquered by their fashions; you take their clothes and they will steal your hearts". And again Ariovistus, sounding like Luther himself: "Your rich squander their wealth, while your poor freeze and starve"; and the king once more: "He who has traffic with fools must be allowed to wear bells"; while Arminius cautions: "Ravens' and cocks' feathers do not befit the eagle." But as to the use of French speech among Germans, and as to the spicing of German with French terms, Ariovistus retorts: "Do cats learn to bark for the love of a dog?"

Yet, even Philander-Moscherosch falls back on his Latin when he moralizes in the vein of his contemporary fellow-writers Grimmelshausen[15] and Rist: "Perfer et obdura". "Dolor hic tibi proderit olim". "Calamitas enim virtutis occasio est. Igitur pelle pusillanimitatem." Then again he comforts his readers in the Lutheran spirit and diction: "Leiden ist heilig" (suffering sanctifies).

However, the best part from the literary point of view is the concluding fable of the search for the biggest fool, in which the 'à-la mode' fool wins the prize of the golden apple.

We have noticed that there is a new note in Moscheroch's treatment of the Arminius theme in conjunction with that of the other visions from the German past. Before Moscherosch, the hero from the past stands, purely and simply, for *personal* heroism, as a challenge and a symbol of national unity and freedom. He reflects everything German as above, or in fair contest with, everything foreign; i.e., he represents highest quality, often even German superiority. In Moscherosch's satire, however, he primarily exposes and attacks present German ills and faults. Here Arminius and his misty companions are set up as stern moral judges of a new generation—as chastisers of their descendants. They reflect the writer's profound concern over the breakdown of his people's old-fashioned stamina and virtues.

Two more versions of the Arminius theme from the last period of the Thirty Years' War deserve attention; one a novel-like chronicle account of the Arminius story and the other a drama with but a brief, though effective, appearance of the Cheruscan hero. The author of the former is Johann Heinrich

Hagelgans; the dramatist is Johannes *Rist,* a spiritual companion of Moscherosch.

The lengthy title of *Hagelgans'* little work sums up its purpose and perspective: "The glorious deeds of the precious prince and defender of German liberty, Arminius. Compiled from Roman sources and rendered into German under the direction of Joh. H. Hagelgans, for the cheerful encouragement of all coming German heroes as well as of other lovers of their country. A map having been added, together with other necessary items. Printed at Wolffgang Enther's, at Nürnberg, in 1640."

For the work was originally written in Latin and then translated under the author's own supervision. It was dedicated to Duke Johann Ernst of Saxony. Again the glorious 'ancestor' Arminius, protector and symbol of German liberty, is recommended to his ducal 'descendant' (and to the reader) for emulation. The author takes his Germans severely to task for having forgotten their national hero for 1500 years. He also is the first one to take issue again with Tacitus', Velleius' and Strabo's interpretations of the characters and motives of Arminius, Varus, Germanicus and others, and emphatically dwells upon the ancient German love of freedom and sense of justice.

However, the most promising feature in Hagelgans' treatment of the Arminius theme is his feeling for human problems and tragedy. Here Arminius and the other heroes stand freed again of their merely type-like status and are returned to human individuality. The author's baroque feeling for psychic tensions enhances his character interpretation and points to the art of a new period.

Johannes *Rist's* drama with the revealing, tragic title of "Peace-wishing Germany" ("Das Friede-wünschende Deutschland"), Nürnberg 1647, was followed five years after the conclusion of the war by another drama entitled "Jubilant Germany" ("Das Friedejauchzende Deutschland"), 1653.

Next to the learned Opitz and the born lyricists Paul Fleming and Paul Gerhardt, Johannes *Rist* was perhaps the most gifted, at least the most influential German poet of his age (1607-'67). A village parson at the very gates of Hamburg all his life, he wielded his pen in an unending mass-production, eagerly harvesting homage and adulation together with his fill of enmity and criticism. A man of uneven temperament and inharmonious nature, he was a figure to arouse hope and controversy from the start. His wide influence was based mainly on the many volumes of religious hymns with which he comforted the hearts of his distracted people. A score of them are still to be found in Protestant hymnals of today. A vain irritability and harshness dwelt within him side by side with sincere feelings, deep sympathy with his fellow men and genuine moral ardor. In the severe features of his rustic physiognomy the sufferings of his generation seem reflected; sufferings of which he himself had to endure his full share. The dreadful experiences of a Philander and a Simplizissimus were also his. Of his many plays, which ranged from biblical and classical topics to the dramatization of men and events of his own age, only four have survived, the two above-mentioned 'Singspiele'[16] among them. Rist mentions some thirty plays as having been lost, stolen or mutilated beyond recognition by war-raids, fire or theft. He himself had tasted plague, shipwreck, flight and utter poverty.

Posterity seems to have appraised him as unevenly as he was received by his contemporaries. But whatever his true literary merit may be, there is no doubt that he had considerable dramatic talent. In the case of our two surviving plays, he put it in the service of his profound moral concern and patriotism. No doubt, he has written these two with the blood of his heart and, perhaps, even as a self-castigation. Mercilessly he exposes the ills of his age, though in a more pastoral vein than Moscherosch did. Like his lay contemporary, Rist labors for the rebirth of a Christian spirit; for humility and tolerance and for a new national consciousness among his people. He too reproaches Germany for being the prime cause of all her sufferings and sees in the misdeeds of her neighbors the plan of an angry God and in the calamitous war a well-deserved purgatory for his wayward nation. In short, in spite of their occasional farcical features, these plays are Lenten sermons delivered on the stage. Their effect was far-reaching and profound.

Rist tells us that he wrote "Das Friede-wünschende Deutschland" to order, for the Hamburg stage and within eight days. That in itself is proof of the author's technical skill and poetic imagination; the more so as its highly allegorical nature would have dissipated the dramatic tension and tragic effect in the hands of a less gifted writer.

The idea of presenting Germany—not only in picture scenes but in successive dramatic stages—as before, during and after the great war, was a bold undertaking. The nation appears personified as 'Queen Germany': Stage I displays her fame, her vain pride and temptation; Stage II her fall, her humiliation and sufferings; Stage III her repentance, her re-birth in spirit and her new elevation before God and the world.

It is obvious that the basic motif is a contest between the forces of Good and Evil. That brings the play close to its medieval forerunners on the stage, but it also lifts it into the spiritual climate of 'Faust,' especially in view of its treatment of the motif of redemption by Divine grace.

The contest between Good and Evil takes place outwardly before the Queen's throne, inwardly within her heart.

Mercury—doubtless a Hutten reminiscence again—and Peace are here the messengers of God; 'Wollust' (lust; licentiousness), followed by Mars, Hunger and Plague, are the instruments of Evil as the immediate sources of Germany's tribulations. The representatives of foreign nations at her court reveal themselves in the course of the play as tools in the wise designs of God. They are Germany's God-sent torturers and tempters, despite their revolting machinations. Thus it is God himself—a God of wrathful retribution—who wills this murderous war in order to arouse, chastise and humble this Germany and, in the end, to purify her proud, degraded, obstinate soul. For, has not the Queen herself driven Peace in anger from her throne because she could not bear the words of Truth? Therewith she has handed herself over to 'Wollust' and sin. Not until her soul is ready to embrace Peace in all humility, will War, Hunger and Plague relent.

Yet, in spite of all her wounds and sufferings, this Queen cannot and must not die, for Germany's soul is immortal. But her worst agonies beset her when the symbol of national unity, the golden chain of 'Concordia', is wrested from her neck: national disunity is Germany's mortal enemy. It is this inner discord, above all, which turns the Queen, once proud and envied, into a bleeding, beggarly wretch tottering on the brink of death.

But what about the Arminius theme and the rôle of the pre-Christian hero in this belated morality play in which a war-torn Germany repents and appears as a humbled supplicant before her angry God?

Again it is Mercurius who introduces the play by singing old Germany's praises. He announces the shades of the past and guides them to the upper-world. And again they are four: king Ariovistus (king 'Ehrenfest': firm-in-honor, as he is often called in the literature of that time) Arminius, Prince Claudius Civilis, and Duke Widukint of Saxony, of the days of Charlemagne. Ariovistus leads again. When Arminius cautions his companions against the Romans, Mercurius proudly asserts that, now, the Germans are ruling the Romans, as for 800 years no 'welsch' king has held sway over Germany(!). The heroes are delighted and desire to see this new nation, while Ariovistus wishes to get one more glimpse of the Germany he once knew.

Then the long series of allegorical 'visions' begins which are to carry the events of the play from stage to stage and bring home to the audience the shocking discrepancies between the new Germany and that of old.

Mercurius plainly warns the visiting shades that they will find a different nation. The climax in their experience is reached with their appearance before new Germany's throne. There the Queen dismisses the pleading warners as fools and impostors. Her anger knows no bounds: In the contest between 'Wollust' and Peace, 'Wollust' has successfully advanced her cause. Soon she will triumph completely when Peace, too, is driven from this court to make room for Mars and his grim companions, Hunger and Plague. With a stern moral rebuke on the part of Mercurius—the messenger of a Christian God—addressed to the recalcitrant Queen whom this new Savonarola calls an "epicurean despiser of God," the rôle of the shades from the past is fulfilled. With the flight of Peace the first Act ends and the humiliation and sufferings of Germany are about to begin.

The play consists of 3 Acts plus an 'Interlude.' But even this Interlude is not a comedy which relieves the distressing mood of the main play but is drawn into the mood and purpose of the whole. In a series of well-chosen and moving 'visions', which reflect the horrors and results of war, it depicts the temptations of German youth allegorically represented by the boisterous and somewhat farcical figure of immature 'Sausewind' (Whirlwind). By Mars he is strongly drawn towards the adventurous immorality of war; while Mercurius, his old teacher, leads him back onto the path of sound judgment, of moral righteousness and Christian living: the regeneration in spirit of Germany's youth is a prerequisite for national and moral recovery.

The remainder of the play is but a series of relentless pictures of Germany's unceasing sufferings—pictures which, in their merciless realism, rival the starkest of the fire-and-brimstone sermons of 17th-century clerical imagination. Finally the catharsis is achieved in the presence of the Almigthy, when Mercurius and Peace have interceded; when Justice has spoken and Love has pleaded her cause; when—by way of a final test— at least the *Hope* of future peace is finally granted to the hard-tried penitent by a merciful God and the shining raiment of Divine Pity is placed upon Germany's poor nakedness.

Her moving prayer of thanks and a hymn of praise on the part of the angels bring the play to its triumphal conclusion.

We have come to the end of this brief survey of a period which opened with such encouraging promises and which ends in disheartening gloom. We have seen what becomes of Tacitus' grandiose Arminius picture—how little survives of his superb mode of treatment of historic themes and tragic human problems.

Already with Hutten we could feel the polemic undercurrent. The century after him, under the impact of cataclysmic political and social events, turned predominantly didactic. That created an unfavorable atmosphere for free artistic creation and interpretation. Only in religious and moral literature, in popular lyrics—and gradually also in religious music—could the national spirit take wing and soar above the sufferings of the day.

Thus, with reference to the Arminius treatment too, we have to look towards a later age and a new generation, before we can hope again for an interpretation worthy of the Tacitean heritage.

Yet we have seen the re-awakened national emotions quite clearly reflected as they range from a naively boastful and even arrogant self-assertion all the way over to deep patriotic sorrow, moral contrition, and self-humiliation.

German national consciousness of the 16th and 17th centuries is largely the product of the activities of academic circles. It stems from the psychic center of the coming nation. Imported from foreign lands, it soon discovers its own worth, its own past and, with it, its own future tasks and possibilities. From there it reaches out, upward towards the social upper-stratum and down to the masses of the people, awakening—for better and for worse—their common national consciousness and hopes.

IV. BAROQUE ROMANTICISM.

'Magnanimous' Hero.

The noted author of a comprehensive History of German Literature of two generations ago[1] had only this to say concerning Daniel Caspar von Lohenstein's (1635-'83) formless "Arminius" novel: "Lohenstein made the liberator of Germany and his Thusnelda the center of a voluminous political, amorous and heroic story ('Staats-, Liebes-und Heldengeschichte') which appeared in 1689 in two quartoes of 3076 pages. In it he has mixed into one indigestible porridge a mass of erudition—historical, antiquarian, geographic and ethnological—together with a masked history of the Hapsburg emperors and of the modern religious wars; plus a patriotically distorted, Germanic primeval history ('Urgeschichte') coupled with Roman, Armenian and Thracian events, in addition to all kinds of philosophy."

That, in broadest outline, circumscribes the material content of this controversial literary hybrid. But the critic, Wilhelm Scherer, utterly ignores the novel's unique importance for the study of baroque thought and of the psychic crisis in the 17th-Century European view of life and fate which Lohenstein's work reflects so strikingly.

Seventeenth Century German literature in particular was too long the step-child of literary historians. Thanks to the efforts of men like Wilhelm Dilthey[2] and other more recent scholars, our understanding of this vital phase in the history of the modern mind has been deepened and corrected considerably.

Luise Laporte[3], in a penetrating study of Lohenstein, terms this "Arminius" the most important 'polite' novel of the 17th century; a psychic mirror of its age; an ultimate climax of the Baroque. This seems to do better justice to the mental world of Lohenstein, who was an ardent student of contemporary European thinkers and himself the German translator of Balthasar Gracian.

I. E. Riffert[4], too, takes a much more tolerant and sympathetic view when he points out the patriotic merits of this novel, which developed so slowly in so unpatriotic an age; which remained unfinished and was not published until six years after the author's death, having been completed by another pen, presumably according to the original plan. Riffert furthermore stresses the undeniable fact that, despite its baroque spirit and romantic garb, this Arminius still remains the brave "defender of German freedom" as he is again set up for emulation, though this time for the benefit of 'polite' Seventeenth Century noblemen, and by the labors of a convinced aristocrat and enlightened absolutist. No doubt, Lohenstein strives to combine the useful with the pleasurable. His thirst for knowledge and mental stimulus appears to be insatiable. And as he absorbs, so he has to pass his knowledge on to others. He must instruct, discuss and educate even while telling exciting love-adventures. Speaking, thus, at once as poet and educator, he also strives to arouse a new patriotic fervor and a moral resurgence in his exhausted nation.

Still, the atmosphere has changed. The buoyant vitality of the 16th century is gone, and the Germany of before 1618 seems all but forgotten. Thus, with Lohenstein's "Arminius" version, we enter into a totally different world and face a new psychic climate: though this "Arminius", too, is not altogether without its mental forebears among the German humanists. For this amorphous attempt at a 'total' novel which strives to embrace all the arts actually reminds one of a romanticized version of the humanists' dream of a *"Germania illustrata"*—a descriptive 'total' history.

Like some humanists before him, Lohenstein ventures to attribute about every excellence in Western history to German effort, to German contributions and ingenuity; like them, he attempts to relate the distant Germanic past to his own distraught age. Once, Thomas Murner had ridiculed the patriotic fantasies of his humanist contemporaries who, in the garb of history, had aimed at the enhancement of German glory, sometimes at the expense of historical accuracy. For they too were dreaming of a German rehabilitation in history, of Germany's aggrandizement at the expense of her "welsch" neighbors. Like the humanists, Lohenstein charges the ancient historians with intentional neglect[5] and with misrepresentation of Germany's historic greatness; with anti-German bias out of envy—while he himself falls victim to gross and intentional patriotic prejudice. Yet there is one marked difference in degree: what, with most humanists, appears to be a rather well-tempered endeavor born of youthful patriotic zeal has, in Lohenstein's case, turned most acutely and even painfully sophistical. The humanists' keen thirst for knowledge—their quest for German heroes—

becomes, in this "Arminius" version, an arrogant historical polymathy which poses as erudition despite its fantastic violence. Moreover, throughout there seems to be perceptible an insurmountable discrepancy between this poet's dream-people and human actuality. The humanists' good-natured enthusiasm for their newly-won national hero now widens into a presumptuous quest for an age-old national culture and heroism—for *the heroic nation par excellence*. That meant, indeed, a considerable step forward in the direction of an intolerant nationalism at any cost[6].

Yet this sophistical coupler of history and fiction, who often proves to be a most delightful story-teller, never claimed to be a writer of "history," but rather a setter of highest human standards as he propagates the personal and social ideals of his soul-searching age. Here life *is* no longer interpretable in the terms of a medieval purgatory, nor is it related to, and anchored in, the purposes of a divine beyond. Nor is life to be experienced any more as a glorious challenge, as the men of the Renaissance were able to take it. The spirit of the medieval *memento mori*, like that of Hutten's triumphant *juvat vivere*, seems far removed indeed. Life has become too complex and far too problematical for both these attitudes. The *inner* man is now man's chief problem, felt with an acute and tragic sense of fate. The novel's psychic temper may well be summed up in the words of Hamlet's player-king:

Our wills and fates do so contrary run,
That our devices still are overthrown;
Our thoughts are ours, their ends none of our own.

Thus Lohenstein could not possibly have been satisfied with relating his own heroic version of the primitive Cheruscan according to "historical sources," though, time and again, he displays an intimate knowledge of Hutten, Velleius, Tacitus and others, even making skilful use of their individual motifs and situations, with often almost literal quotations. His personal interest in the hero who was to lend his name to this incongruous compilation of adventures is actually quite remote. He too is used as a mask through which to express the baroque ideal of human heroism in the face of an inscrutable fate, the ideal of human perfection. This hero's predominant virtue is *Grossmut*: the *magna anima*, greatness and beauty of soul. This *Grossmut* in action is the novel's basic theme. Just as behind the fancied genealogy of the Cheruscan 'rulers' stands the story of the Hapsburg dynasty, and behind Arminius the figure of the author's emperor, Leopold, so—throughout the story—historical events of the distant past and of Europe's more recent history run parallel and blend. This intentional display of learning and abuse of facts, this telescoping and double-play of historic figures and events, earned the author the admiration and delight of his baroque contemporaries everywhere, but also the wrath of later critics, who stigmatized his mode of treatment as *Geschichtsklitterung*—a wilful garbling and distorting of history.

But why did the author give the name of Arminius at all to this mass of loosely connected events from all the corners of the earth and of history? Because, as a tribute and challenge to his nation, this Arminius was to be set up as *the* hero of heroes. He was to represent, in every respect, the highest qualities of the author's conception of human integrity, of inner greatness and perfection of character. All other heroes and heroines—and they are many—seem to receive their rank from their relation to this hero's steadfastness of soul, tested in the most trying adversities of earthly existence.

The introduction to the second and last edition of *Arminius*[7] elucidates the point as it states: "Lohenstein only wrote for his own and his friends' entertainment. He had not thought of publication. People of quality ('von Stand') do not like to read. Therefore the author spiced his love-stories with useful and serious elements, political and moral. He intended to lead the reader onto the path of virtue without compulsion and in a playful manner, as he also wished to arouse aversion for bad books."

That states it clearly: Lohenstein wishes to stimulate the interest of his badly informed co-noblemen by letting them taste of his own prodigious knowledge and thought. He strives to keep their curiosity alive by sheer bulk of adventure and exciting changes in fortunes. The editor then adds that Lohenstein also intended "to demonstrate the effects of goodness and the consequences of evil; the inner rewards of virtue and the punishments of vice"[8].

As to the relation of the novel's heroes to their prototypes in history, the editor offers the following caustic remark: "If the heroes of the distant past could see themselves in this novel, they probably would be surprised that their gross ('dick') barbarism has been metamorphosed by the Ovidius of our times into a pattern of modern good breeding and of our way of life ('Lebensart'); that he has transformed them—not from human beings into animals, but from half-animals into perfect (genteel) human beings"[9].

It follows that the author's attitude and purpose were obvious to the intelligent contemporary readers who shared his tastes. Like them, we should read this "Arminius" as excursions into the fields of 17th century political, cultural and moral speculations. The author of such tendencies must have had little taste, indeed, for primitive communities and their stalwart heroes. The lure of pre-cultural vigor and youthfulness—the vigor that once had captivated and disturbed a Tacitus—was utterly lost to Lohenstein. Conversely Lohenstein's heart obviously is with the utmost in cultural luxury, with all the *raffinement* and *décadence* which he pretends to condemn so vehemently. Actually, he forces his virtuous pre-cultural community towards that dazzling sphere while feigning to contrast the simple, stalwart virtues of the one with the effeminate snares and sinful aberrations of the other. Compared with Lohenstein, all his forerunners in the field of our Arminius literature, Moscherosch included—though with the one exception of the belated Roman, Tacitus—appear to be thoroughly *'naive,'* while Lohenstein is *'sentimentalisch'* in the sense of Schiller's succinct antithesis of these terms. He represents, as the first since Tacitus, the hyperconscious, highly reflective type who cannot but suffer from the world while pondering the meaning of life, of human happiness and fate. For he feels deeply that man is controlled by inscrutable natural forces which overwhelm him as he cannot deflect them. In a sense, Lohenstein forms a bridge from Luther's faith to Schiller's moral world. Here, Luther's stern, incomprehensible God recedes in order to re-enter, secularized and without mercy, in the rôle of an awesome fate. ('das verehrungswürdige, furchtbare Verhängnis'). This stern power permeates Lohenstein's world as an unfathomable force which man must fear and revere. His only way to rise above it is by submitting, voluntarily and absolutely, to its guidance and decree.

On the other hand, Lohenstein's philosophy of life shares in the social double-morale of his class—its aristocratic, individualistic aloofness and prejudice: Quod licet Jovi, non licet bovi. Here the privileged noble, center and purpose of his well-ordered social world—there the chaotic, vulgar crowd, the *'Pöfel.'*

However, behind this egocentric, intolerant social contrast stands another one; a deeper, even more individualistic—because much rarer and much more ethical—antithesis: here the few inwardly free, the 'Grossmütigen' whose will and superior judgment have come to govern their passions (their 'Affekte'); there the inwardly unfree, the slaves of whims, of vulgar, selfish desire. Thus Lohenstein's aristocratic class prerogative also reflects the fastidious choice of superior ethical personality and inner independence. For Lohenstein's heroes—all aristocrats by birth or breeding—are, in turn, divided among themselves into 'Grossmütige' and those who are and remain but 'passion's slaves.' Though it can not be denied that, at least in this "Arminius" novel, the 'Grossmütige' are predominantly on the German side and their less fortunate opposites in the foreign camp, there still are noble exceptions among Romans and Orientals alike. The highest aims of their ideal type (first of all Arminius himself, then his few notable rivals for this austere distinction) may well be summed up in Hamlet's moving plea when, in his perilous position and out of tragic inner loneliness, he flies to Horatio's heart[10]

—for thou hast been
As one, in suffering all, that suffers nothing,
A man that fortune's buffets and rewards
Hast ta'en with equal thanks; and *blessed are those
Whose blood and judgment are so well co-mingled
That they are not a pipe to fortune's finger
To sound what stop she please. Give me that man
That is not passion's slave,—*

Here, in the small confines of the corrupt Danish court, we have the agitated world of Lohenstein anticipated; and as in "Hamlet," so in this "Arminius" novel: not the *outer* conflicts, not the actions, intrigues and fortuitous events—massive though they may be—give the plot its true meaning, but the *inner* conflicts with their everlasting psychic tests and tensions in which the hero suffers, proves himself and sometimes triumphs. Thus both reflect a keen awareness of the underlying tragedy within the individual personality itself.

Here we have penetrated to the core of Lohenstein's thought and view of life, which seem to center upon the interplay of 'blood and judgment'—of passion, knowledge, happiness and fate. Lohenstein's thought points both backward to the Socratic world and Stoa and forward to 18th-Century Enlightenment. The Socratic moral formula of knowledge=virtue=happiness (from knowledge through virtue to lasting inner peace)—of which Archytas at the close of Wieland's novel "Agathon"[11] affords such a striking example—presupposes knowledge as the understanding and mastery of self. But it also demands action: the testing of its worth in the fires of life, together with the moral mastery of others. This is the truly heroic *doer*-type. Lohenstein's Arminius figure is meant to represent him at his peak. But this novel also shows the other side, the heroic doer's counterpart: the pure and tranquil thinker, the *hermit*-type and seer who withdraws from life, who contemplates it with serenity. His one remaining task is to instruct others in the true art of virtuous living[12]. Thus Lohenstein's Ariovistus (among a score of hermits in this novel) retreats, Faust-like, to cave and wilderness. Here he matures into a selfless benefactor and spiritual guide of men. In this way he complements Arminius himself, though, ideally, the perfect hero type is to embrace both thought *and* action, self-assertion *and* renunciation, in a well-balanced way as the pattern of utmost human attainment. Once achieved, it signifies man's inner triumph over fate. Thus even in the agitated world of Lohenstein, ruled outwardly by stringent formalism and absolute conventionality, the individual still can rise—through discipine of self and constant readiness for renunciation—to genuine peace of mind and a truly noble inner freedom.

With the final achievement of this "sacred tranquillity" within the self, which the hermit represents and preaches and few other mortals attain, man contributes to the will and plan of the Maker: to the "perfect inner harmony of all things created."[13] With this cosmic view Lohenstein links himself to the mystic wisdom of saints and sages; a view which, in the end, does promise an earthly salvation to a select few among his storm-tossed human beings.

We have tried to delineate briefly the nature of Lohenstein's ideal hero, which can be done only by way of approximation. For, nowhere in this novel filled with courageous people does this "perfect" hero actually appear in a "pure" state. Nevertheless, the ideal can be deduced from the behavior and actions of the major characters, with Arminius in the lead; but above all from those interminable psychological and moral discussions that fill the story to its final page. Moreover, it must be remembered that these heroic adventure-tales are told by a pessimist whose accounts often ring with the fatalist's ironic laughter. Again and again he threatens, by preposterous postulates and assertions, to turn his picture of stately pageantry into a semi-travesty.

Thus it is not accidental that Lohenstein also shows the romanticist's psychic disharmony and inner ambiguity in his attitude towards his distant hero with his "ancient" culture. As the author himself is firmly rooted in contemporary 'welsch'-baroque culture, his attitude towards the primitive is full of psychological contradictions, and irony remains as his last resort. Yet irony and scepticism are the very antipodes of all naive vitality.

The basic discrepancy thus remains, since baroque moral philosophy and youthful tribal urge and vigor do not blend. The aristocratic stoic's maxim of "being born a prince, of living as a hero, and dying a sage" sound strange, indeed, in the mouth of a Teutonic king Marcomir[14].

A brief survey of the technical and thematic aspects of Lohenstein's Arminius version reveals a rough resemblance to the old King Arthur legend-pattern: a group of heroes, each with his individual purposes and Odyssean adventures which at some point in time converge at the "court" of one superior central figure—there King Arthur, here both Arminius and the emperor at Rome. But with one basic difference: though in this "Arminius," too, the figures are in some measure held together by common cultural standards and the ideals of their caste, they still vary considerably in point of *moral* quality and purpose. We have pointed out that these heroes fall into two basic moral categories: the *"Grossmütige"* and their counterparts, the *"Wankelmütige"*—the few great models of self-discipline, of moral integrity and perfect chivalry of heart; and the self-possessed, graded downward from the merely weak ones to the downright wicked: the host of traitors, opportunists, self-seekers and intriguers for egotistic ends.

Even the noblewomen of this story, with true heroines among them, are similarly classifiable and graded as the noble-hearted and the evil, selfish schemers.

To cull the Arminius story proper from the rest of this gigantic mass of subject-matter, and to order the whole into a coherent sequence (or proper parallel developments), is in itself a Gargantuan task. To trace the major motives of the manifold adventures to their respective "sources" would prove completely futile with a writer who absorbs facts, ideas and every kind of stimuli from all corners of history and from the seven seas of life. Last but not least: this Arminius story is but a pretext for fabling freely and for moralizing (tongue in cheek) along the lines of a Utopian German history.

Of the 18 books which make up this novel in two volumes of originally 9 books each[15], only about four concern themselves directly—though in parts only—with Arminius' own heroic exploits. In passages of other books, his youth and earlier accomplishments are told by others. Hence, the Arminius story proper fills but a part of the entire novel, the bulk of which comprises the exploits and adventures of figures more or less directly related to the central hero and his fate. The very essence of the book, however, is and remains the dialogue—the theoretical discussion of social standards, of moral principles and values, as exemplified by human will in action.

Book I, which opens with the Walpurgis *motif*—the suicide of a virtuous and helpless German princess pursued by the corrupt seducer Varus—here the immediate (and moral!) cause of the general revolt which finally leads to German freedom—sets the major political theme for the heroic novel right at the start: *rather dead than a slave*! For various reasons, it is the most important book of all and ought to be the last, as it contains the Varus battle—the climactic contest between Germany and Rome—to which the others are like preludes in reverse, enlarged commentaries or aftermaths. Moreover, it is filled with the familiar men and motives, both political and human. Here is Varus, again voluptuous, covetous, haughty, easy-going, readily deceived and neglectful of duty. There is the 'wankelmütige' Segestes, a selfish, jealous, traitorous intriguer, ready to gamble with his children's fate for his own power and preferment. There are, moreover, the heroic women, Ismene, the hero's sister, and Thusnelda, his beloved but not yet betrothed. They take part in disguise in the decisive battle which brings Segestes, deserter in disguise, into actual combat with his valiant daughter. Yet it is Thusnelda who saves him from his just desert at the hands of the high priest when she offers to sacrifice herself in atonement for his shameful treason and for her breach of filial loyalty. This noble deed leads to her betrothal at the priest's request, but also to Segestes' undying jealousy and hate of his future son-in-law and rival. For Arminius is here again the prime champion of revenge, of revolt and liberty. In personal combat he encounters Varus, whose voluntary death after his ignominious defeat earns him again the dubious Roman epitaph: "more courage in death than in battle."

There is furthermore King Marobod, the fickle "friend of Rome," together with Inguiomerus and Adgandester (here a high officer and chief steward at Arminius' court). Both are brave and loyal at the first but *'wankelmütig'* in their hearts and future deadly enemies of the Cheruscan leader, and for most selfish ends.

Finally there are the well-drawn, fictitious representatives of Eastern culture, Zeno and Erato, the Armenian prince and princess (brother and sister, though not yet known as such to one another), whom fate has led by various routes into the Roman camp, and into German captivity. On them, above all others, Arminius and his people are to practice their exemplary *'Grossmut,'* rewarded at the story's end with Flavius' marriage to the beautiful Armenian queen and Ismene's union with the hero Zeno.

Most of these leading figures—including Arminius' mother, the heroic and saintly but legendary Asblaste—and Flavius, his brother, form in turn centers of special adventure-cycles and weird Odysseys subsequently related. Thus we have in this novel, beside the lengthy story of the central hero, the comprehensive tales of Asblaste and her husband, Segimer; of Flavius, of Ismene and Thusnelda, of Zeno and Erato, and of a host of minor figures. Basically, they all reflect the same human experiences and trials, though with altering color and locale.

However, in this type of novel it should hardly surprise the reader that individuality gives way considerably to types, i.e., to the embodying of human virtues, weaknesses, and vice. There are, moreover, the frequent psychological inconsistencies on the part of many of these "characters," especially, of course, among the representatives of human frailty—the *'Wankelmütige.'* There are, for instance, Flavius and Sigismund (son of Segestes) who now abduct Thusnelda and her children[16] for the Romans and then again assist them in escaping from their captivity; they are forever changing sides. One is tempted to ask: have such human beings no principles at all, no convictions nor personal attachment?

The two major human passions depicted in this novel are ambition for power and renown, and love. They occur in a hundred variations, from delicate, half-hidden emotions to the point of devastating fury.

Still, at the bottom of this Arminius version, too, lie all the basic themes and motives of our former Roman sources, though encrusted with the author's lavish fancy, i.e., romantically enhanced or inflated.

There is again, as in Velleius, Tacitus, and Hutten, the grandiose political contest between Germany and Rome—though with a decided bent towards national equality (or even German superiority) by virtue of supposed ancient historical and cultural achievements, plus a superior moral quality. There are, moreover, the tragic feuds in families—though this time with a melodramatic "happy ending" for Arminius and Thusnelda, for Flavius and Erato, Zeno and Ismene, and for some others who happen to survive and withstand the "slings and arrows of outrageous fortune." Again we find the tragic inner division among German tribes which Arminius attempts so valiantly—though mostly unsuccessfully—to reconcile; which he himself, however, weathers and survives. His attempts at unifying Germany call forth the violent rivalry of Segestes and king Marobod and prompt the endless intrigues of their evil tools, Sentia, the scheming Roman and second wife of Segestes, and also of Inguiomerus and Adgandester. These selfish plots and quarrels often endanger concerted action, or even destroy the fruits of victory. Yet above them all triumphs in the end the *Grossmut* of Arminius and Thusnelda and, with it, their magnificent, undaunted love.

On the other hand, the rivalry between the usurper Marobod and the honorable Arminius concerns here not only the hegemony over Germany, but even the possession of Thusnelda herself. For through Segestes' selfish machinations Thusnelda has been promised, in turn, to Arminius, to Tiberius and Marobod. Arminius himself has to rescue her more than once from shipwreck, capture, imprisonment and even from imminent murder. And as Thusnelda is besieged by her three unequal wooers, so Arminius' life is plotted against by at least three of his mortal foes; for, to the Tacitean plot by Adgandester there are added the dagger-and-poison attempts of Segestes and Tiberius.

Moreover, embedded in these endless Odysseys and "comedies of errors" with the recurrent separations and reunions of relatives and lovers, behind these never-ending disguises of men as women and women as men, often lie truly tragic psychic tensions that vex the souls of the worthiest of these heroes and heroines. There is, above all, Thusnelda's anguish, torn as she is between her filial obedience and devotion to a dishonorable, wicked parent and her love for the hero of her heart. But there is also her protracted mental anguish when she is pursued by Marobod in Germany and by the lascivious Tiberius in Rome. Her sufferings during her guilded Roman captivity are almost literal repetitions of those endured before by Asblaste at Augustus' court; just as the trials, temptations and heroic exploits of Arminius at that corrupted seat of power are paralleled by those of Flavius, his brother. Last, but not least, the tragic theme of the inner division within families, of which each seems to have its share of *Grossmütige* and of many frailer members, appears in the house of Arminius, in the family of Segestes, of Marobod and others whose stories are told incidentally. Rare, indeed, are the cases where two *Grossmütige* form a completely harmonious pair untrammeled by some wicked kin as, in the end, Arminius and Thusnelda themselves. The noble couple of Germanicus and Agrippina represent the Roman virtues and civilized humaneness at their very peak; they and the hapless Sentius Saturninus, the noble father of the wretched sinner, Sentia, form a bridge of understanding and good will across all human baseness, hate and passion.

But above all these harrowing pictures of humanity engulfed in violence and fate shines again the Hutten-Tacitus *motif*: "When all other nations had succumbed to the power of Rome, the Germans alone were yet free"—divided though they remain among themselves when the immediate danger has passed. And to the Tacitean appraisal of Arminius: "overcome in battle—unconquered in war"—a compliment which Lohenstein, no doubt, wishes to extend inferentially to his heroic nation—this author, like Hutten before him, adds the other even more heroic and much more glorious one: *he conquered himself!*

The spread of the Arminius theme to the literatures of Germany's neighbors begins at about the middle of the 17th century. During Lohenstein's youth the broad flow of French baroque novels into Germany had begun. In 1645, *Zesen* translated Madelaine de *Scudéry's* novel "Ibrahim." Conversely, at about that time Arminius makes his debut on the stage of France with Georges de *Scudéry's* tragi-comedy "Arminius, ou les frères ennemis," in 1643.

As the title indicates, the *motif* of the hostile brothers, Arminius and Flavian, gives rise to the drama with the contest between Rome and Germany (Germanicus-Arminius) lending an important though remotely felt background to the action. It plays after the Varus battle. However, Flavian's reason for his hostility is not at all political conviction but his sudden love for Hercinie (Thusnelda), his brother's fiancée, whom he has played into Roman hands. He hopes to estrange her from Arminius and then win her for himself. He thus takes over part of Ségeste's functions in the older Arminius versions. Ségeste, again his fickle, arrant self, is quite eager to accept this second suitor for his daughter behind Arminius' back. Arminius, however, finally succeeds in freeing his tormented fiancée and brings about a reconciliation between Flavian and Ségimire, the loyal former beloved of his fickle brother.

The play opens with Hercinie's captivity. Her resolute resistance to Ségeste's and Flavian's plot, rewarded with her final rescue by Arminius, forms the high point of the dramatic events. Again Ségeste advises the Roman general—this time it is not Varus but Germanicus—to capture the valiant leader of the rebellious Germans. This the Roman refuses to do, as "fighting the enemy with fraud and hate" is disgraceful in the eyes of the Roman nobleman.[17] Conversely, the cunning Ségeste tries to refute this lofty view by calling such a crime a mere political expedience.

Here *Grossmut* is about evenly divided among the high-minded Roman leader, Germanicus, and the heroic and patriotic Germans, Arminius, Hercinie and Ségimire, whereas selfishness and treachery are on the side of the intriguers, Ségeste and Flavian—the *'Wankelmütige.'* It is Hercinie who separates the hostile brothers when Flavian attacks Arminius, who has come to the Roman camp in good faith in order to offer precious Roman trophies from the Varus battle in exchange for his fiancée's freedom; and while Germanicus prompts Hercinie to choose between the rival brothers, it is Arminius who, in turn, re-unites the former lovers, Flavian and his faithful Ségimire.

Thus this "Arminius" version, too, depicts a family drama put in motion by selfish intrigues, though with a political background. Yet, its major theme is not at all Germany's fate and freedom, but the freeing and regaining of a beloved woman. There is little left, indeed, of the broad range of the Tacitean plot with its world-wide implications. Though the play contains some gripping episodes and rapid action, the tragic psychic tensions of the Roman sources have given way to mere anxious suspense created from without, while the heroic courage of one man and of two steadfast women prevails in the end over the selfish designs of their unnatural enemies.

In 1685, two years after Lohenstein's early death, there appeared on the Paris stage a second Arminius drama which was played 29 times between the years of 1684 and 1709. The author of it was Jean-Galbert *Campistron*.

Whereas de Scudéry had chosen the conflict between Arminius and Germanicus as a background for his family intrigue, Campistron depicts again the earlier conflict between Arminius and Varus with the latter's sudden defeat and violent end. However, while he follows Tacitus' report in many of his details, he, like Lohenstein, makes the Roman general (here Varus and not Tiberius) a suitor of Isménie (Thusnelda), thus twisting the vast theme of the contest for German freedom into a love-triangle play, with a consequent shrinkage of its former grandiose proportions.

It may be assumed that Lohenstein was familiar with the work of both the Scudérys as well as with the novels of La Calprenède, Campistron's main source for his Arminius play. Here Lohenstein found the atmosphere of his own novel anticipated: this world of heroic adventures and achievements, of stately pageantry and cunning disguises, with its ever-recurrent abductions and liberations and the loves of heroic couples beset by an adverse fate; this aristocratic milieu with its theatrical rhetoric and fustian, didactic diction in which the hero, in the end, becomes a mouth-piece for the moralizing author himself.

Campistron, too, used his sources quite freely and made out of their varicolored elements a drama of love and patriotism, with the final emphasis on the latter. Ségeste, again a traitor to his country, has brought his daughter, Isménie, into the Roman camp. Despite her engagement to Arminius, he is about to marry her to the elderly Roman general, Varus, disregarding her vigorous opposition. His son's engagement to Arminius' sister (Sigismond-Polixène) still stands, however.

Thus we have this time the theme of a double engagement between the two rival families. Before Arminius arrives in the Roman camp in order to rescue his fiancée, he has cautiously assembled his army in the woods about the camp: to such minor proportions has the fateful Varus battle shrunk in this Campistron version! In due time—after a highly dramatic dialogue between Arminius and Ségeste concerning their patriotic duties as leaders of the Germans—Ségeste arrests Arminius and urges Varus to have the Cheruscan killed on the spot. But the Roman again refuses. He intends to leave the captive's fate to Rome. Now it is Sigismond's love for Arminius' sister that gives to the plot its sudden decisive turn: Sigismond forsakes his father and the Roman side. He secretly frees Arminius and has him spirited away, after Varus himself had intercepted the German's first attempt to flee the camp. While Ségeste makes ready to take Arminius and his children away to Rome, word comes of the Roman defeat and of Varus' violent death. Then Arminius enters as victor. Ségeste, now his captive, pleads to be killed at once. But he is promptly freed and forgiven, and the way is cleared for the union of the faithful couples and Germany's freedom seems once more assured.

Hence Ségeste appears again as the selfish villain. Yet Arminius intends to win him back to the cause of German unity by personal magnanimity and kindness. Nevertheless, the elderly, irresolute Varus remains an unconvincing and unheroic figure, as a leader as well as a lover. Moreover, we are asked to believe that the outcome of the history-making Varus battle is to depend largely on the patriotic challenge of one woman (Polixène) and on her suitor's (Sigismond's) prompt return to the German side for the sake of her love. Of course, the battle and its outcome are also rooted in Varus' indecision when confronted with the final fate of his captured rival in arms and in love. His underestimation of Arminius' character and stamina was well founded in the Roman sources. Yet the fact remains that it is Polixène's attitude which, above all else, makes the decisive battle even possible.

While Campistron's drama is not without dramatic moments and suspense, it could easily take place anywhere and at any time with a few changes in names and locale. This could be said of Scudéry's play as well. And while Ségeste's fate has its tragic aspect, there is little left of the heroic resistance of a vigorous, primitive people to the overpowering might of Rome. Rather, a world-historic battle shrinks to the size of a skirmish about a camp in which a leader perishes. Arminius' onslaught upon the Romans is again little more than a desperate attempt to free Isménie, Polyxène, Sigismond, and a handful of his loyal followers caught within the hostile camp. Flavian, however, and with him the theme of the hostile brothers, has disappeared completely. Ségeste alore is the cause of the impending love-tragedy, which is prevented only by the quick foresight of Arminius and Sigismond. The deep-rooted conflict between two German political convictions—peace *under* Rome, or war to the finish *against* her—is thus dissipated in the personal rivalry of unequal lovers who, like their setting, breathe the atmosphere of 17th-Century French Baroque.

With Scudéry and Campistron we have reached the first full-sized Arminius dramas. However, they did not originate in Germany but in France.

To these are to be added a number of contemporary and early 18th century *operas*, Italian as well as German. Here the record is unfortunately incomplete and the librettos, if still extant, are mostly beyond reach.

Lancaster[18] refers to a statement by Campistron in the preface to an edition of his "Arminius," of 1707, in which the French playwright mentions a translation of his drama into Italian and its adaptation for an opera which was "given for 3 months at the court of Tuscany." Lancaster assumes that this "Arminio" opera was produced in 1703 and that the author of its text was the Florentine, Antonio Salvi.

Riffert[19], on the other hand, states that an Arminius opera, now lost, had been performed at Nuremberg as early as 1687; and a second one, in 1697, under the title of "Arminius, the German Arch-hero," which had been arranged by Christof Adam

Naegelein. French-Italian in taste, it was dedicated to Lohenstein's emperor, Leopold, whom it extolled as Germany's new Arminius. Its libretto was partly in alexandrine verse and acknowledged its indebtedness to Campistron.

The music and pageantry-loving 18th century was to produce several more Arminius musical plays (*Singspiele*). Riffert mentions three more which originated between 1725 and '49, two with Arminius and one with Thusnelda in the central rôle. However, the first, which appeared anonymously in 1725, is mentioned by Gottsched in his preface to Schönaich's "Hermann" and may have been a drama with musical interludes. Riffert assumes that it has been lost. The second, a musical drama called "Arminius" (Ital. "Arminio"), was published in Italian and German at Dresden, in 1745, with its text by Joh. C. Pasquini and the music by Joh. Adolf Hassen. The "Thusnelda" *Singspiel* libretto appeared in Leipzig, in 1749, and was composed by a Danish musician, Johann Adolf Scheibe. All three are extremely rare and may even be lost.

Suffice it to point out that the new musical medium, too, must have contributed considerably to the ever-growing popularity of the Arminius theme at home and abroad.[20]

We conclude this brief survey of the age of Lohenstein by mentioning a man who, according to his years, should stand at its beginning. But as to his contribution to the Arminius literature, he is the most modest one of all. He was the leader of the so-called Second Silesian School of Poetry, Christian Hofmann von *Hofmannswaldau* (1617-'79), gifted *protégé* of Martin Opitz, and himself, in turn, the model of his fellow-Silesian, Lohenstein.

Inspired by the work of his follower Lohenstein, Hofmann wrote his inconspicuous Arminius poem[21] in Alexandrine verse. It brings Arminius and Thusnelda together right after the Varus battle. As Thusnelda bids the victor welcome, the courteous hero assures the lady of his heart that not he, but she who had inspired him, deserved the real glory of the victory.

V. TOWARDS A NATIONAL DRAMA.

Culture-Nation.

THE ERA OF J. E. SCHLEGEL AND KLOPSTOCK

Johann Elias *Schlegel* (1718-'49) is the first member of a remarkable family which contributed abundantly to German thought and letters. In several respects Elias' work marks a milestone and a new beginning. Besides being a precursor of Lessing and Schiller in the field of aesthetics, it was he who created the first original German tragedy which departs from the French taste and pattern. This he accomplished with his first play, "Hecuba"[1], at the age of eighteen. It was Schlegel who strove as the first for the establishment of a national theater and for the foundation of stage companies financially independent of the hazards of day-to-day receipts. Here too, he anticipates his great successor, Lessing. Finally, it was Schlegel who gave to the Germans their first full-sized national play in his ingenious "Hermann" drama, which he wrote as a Leipzig student when only twenty-two years old. With it he lent a new popularity to the Arminius theme while also setting a new standard for his numerous successors in the dramatic treatment of this plot. Last but not least: his drama marks a new dawn in German national literature.

The literary scene of Germany was at that time divided into two rival camps: here the academic Gottsched with his mighty retinue, striving to raise German literary taste and to educate German poets by emulating the French example; on the other side the young genius of religious experience and imagination, Klopstock, echoed by his enthusiastic followers. This second group stood for a new national literature based on the freedom of individual experience and emotion while also pointing back to the German cultural past. Above all, they demanded freedom from "welsch" patterns with their stifling rules.

Though writing under the Argus eyes of the dogmatic Gottsched—then Germany's literary oracle and dictator—the young student proved strong enough to learn from the Leipzig professor but not to be detracted. Schlegel had chosen the Arminius theme against Gottsched's wish and advice. Ho proceeded nevertheless and was able to assert his artistic independence to such an extent that, in the end, both rival parties claimed the short-lived poet as one of their own. Gottsched had even published the first version of the "Herrmann" drama[2], though not without distortions which later were corrected. Schlegel's star had risen quite suddenly over the German literary scene, to disappear just as quickly: a setter of new artistic standards, a preparer of new ways towards a new national art.

With Schlegel's "Hermann" drama (1740-'41) we have left behind the varicolored, baroque world of a Lohenstein and his controversial school, and literary figures take on human proportions again. Enthusiasm was running high and literary feuds were fought with vigor. Gottsched never relented in his efforts to quell the vogue of Lohenstein. Klopstock's circle tried in turn, as Lessing did later, to refute the dicta of the Leipzig autocrat in matters of literary form and taste, Gottsched. Yet Schlegel's heart no doubt was with the defenders of irrational, imaginative, and religious poetry, with the anti-French and pro-German literary faction of his day. His drama is German in feeling and spirit. In dramatic effect and genuine poetic beauty it outranks by far the French Arminius versions of Scudéry and Campistron.

Schlegel's "Hermann" drama in five acts contains only 11 speaking persons. Its scene is a sacred grove on the eve of and during the Varus battle. The conflict and rivalry between Segest and Hermann form its major theme. Germany is again divided into prò- and anti-Roman factions. Around Hermann are grouped the freedom-loving allied tribes; while Segest draws his following mainly from the opposition stirred up by him against the newly chosen Cheruscan leader. The hero's parents are the aging patriot, Sigmar, who leaves the leadership to his youthful but battle-tested son, and Adelheid, also a true patriot in spirit. Their second son, Flavius, the Roman-trained partisan of Varus and Segest, seems to become the center of this play more than once. He has fallen in love with Thusnelda, his brother's fiancée. Segest attempts to lure him to his side by promising him his daughter despite her betrothal to Arminius.

Thus we have once more the old motif of the conflict among Germans, even within their leading families, interfering with the political contest between Germany and Rome at the hour of crisis. The house of Sigmar is divided by the rivalry between the sons, Hermann and Flavius. In the house of Segest the treason of Segest himself is challenged by the patriotism of

Thusnelda. This situation is complicated further by the indecision of Siegmund, Segest's son, who wavers between his father's machinations, a Roman priesthood forced upon him, and the natural call of duty to his native land.

However it must be stressed that—with the exception of Flavius, who, in the end, does gain a belated understanding of his neglected duty—love actually plays but a minor part in Schlegel's drama. The main heroes, Hermann and Thusnelda, are ready at any moment to put duty to their country above their personal hopes and wishes. That may give to the play a certain touch of inhuman coldness; but it also lifts the drama to a high ethical level. The struggle between "Pflicht und Neigung"—duty and desire—runs through the entire plot, though this conflict does not occur within the major heroes. As exemplary representatives of public duty, they are Schlegel's 'Grossmütige': Sigmar, who, despite his age, gladly pays the supreme sacrifice in the battle for German freedom, and his equally stout-hearted wife, Adelheid. There is, above all, their heroic older son who, in the person of Segest's noble daughter, has chosen a life-companion worthy of himself. Conversely, there are again the 'Wankelmütige': Flavius, whose selfish passion leads him astray, while he hides his inner conflict behind his conscience-bound "duties" to his foster-country, Rome. There is finally Siegmund, who is torn between the voice of conscience and his scheming father. Hermann and Thusnelda, however, are kept above such psychic conflicts. In them duty reigns supreme.

It is the arrant egotism of Segest which sets the dramatic plot in motion as he attempts to rise over the bodies of friend and foe to the German throne, using the trusting Varus in the process. But precisely this weakness of the foolish Varus also counteracts Segest's betrayal and prevents a German catastrophe before the decisive battle comes about: the Roman leader does not believe the warnings of Segest. He even lets the German leaders go and sets their hostages free—out of contempt for Germany's weakness, we are told with good dramatic effect. This Segest, however, is not even 'wankelmütig' (i.e., really human), but a cruel villain without a trace of conscience: a major psychological weakness of the play which makes itself quite noticeable at the end when, thanks to the "Grossmut" of the victor over Varus, Segest again goes free, while Flavius at least repents in shame. Yet a basic dramatic weakness does remain: the absence of genuine human passion which would involve the real heroes in conflicts with each other or within themselves. Muncker[3] has put his finger on the weak spot when he generalizes with reference to the dramatic treatment of the Arminius plot, "As soon as the poetic presentation is to reach its climax with a victory over Varus dimmed by nothing else, then the epic character of the plot must offer insurmountable difficulties to the dramatic poet. All our Arminius plays, from Schlegel to Grabbe, suffer from this basic defect." It therefore does credit to Schlegel as an artist that his play does not lack altogether in genuine dramatic and human appeal. It is skilfully built up towards its climax with a fine distribution of tension, retardation, and stirring emotions.

It lends a touch of irony to the story of the play if one recalls that it was translated into French by Bauvin under the title of "Arminius," in 1769, and once more, in a freer and modified version, in 1773, under the name of "Les Chérusques." That the conflict between Germany and Rome could easily be interpreted as a mask for the historic German-French rivalry—especially in view of Schlegel's opposition to Gottsched's French-inspired tendencies—seems to have escaped Bauvin and his Paris audience altogether.

Whether or not intended as such, there are reasons to allow for such an interpretation. However, it is not anti-French propaganda in any political sense but rather a declaration of cultural and social independence and, therefore, is akin to the aims of Moscherosch. In that sense it fights on Klopstock's side and, like Klopstock's patriotic works, is a spiritual forerunner of that youthful literary movement of one generation later which has been called "Storm and Stress."

The first four scenes of Schlegel's play elucidate its ideological purpose. Here Sigmar, the patriarchal mentor of his unequal sons and of the divided Germans, anticipates the rôle of that venerable Swiss patriot in Schiller's "Wilhelm Tell," Attinghausen, who also calls a wavering kinsman back to his country's side. For this Rudenz, like Flavius, is drawn to the enemy camp by the love of a woman:

> Ans Vaterland, ans teure, schliess' dich an,
> Das halte fest mit deinem ganzen Herzen!
> Hier sind die starken Wurzeln deiner Kraft;

Dort in der fremden Welt stehst du allein,
Ein schwankes Rohr, das jeder Sturm zerknickt.[4]

In this spirit, Scene 1 of Schlegel's drama shows old Sigmar advising his youthful son about his patriotic duties as the newly chosen leader of his people. He bids him be guided in his actions by those ancient German virtues of love of freedom, love of glory, loyalty, and magnanimity towards friend and foe—in short, by "Grossmut." "Shun treachery, effeminacy and lawlessness" (i.e., tyranny), this Sigmar counsels. "Be your country's shield from enemies and vice"; and, quite in the vein of an enlightened absolutist of the type of Frederick the Great—who ascended the throne of Prussia during the year when this drama was begun—"find your own happiness in the happiness of your people"; i.e., be the first servant of your land and not its lawless master! But, above all else, Sigmar calls upon his son to guard the old German love of simplicity and faithfulness now endangered by the lures of Roman treachery and glittering vice: "gold breeds licentiousness," he warns; and "the Romans bribe with lust and gold." And, sounding like Moscherosch, Rist or Lohenstein, he adds "nowadays innocence is driven out and simplicity is ridiculed." When Sigmar refuses to go to Varus' camp, and when Arminius regrets having been in the service of Rome, we may well interpret these gestures, not as manifestations of undying enmity, but as symbolic declarations of national maturity and cultural independence and, inferentially, as the author's declaration of freedom from Gottsched and his France.

Thus interpreted, the main figures could represent the various stages of such inner independence. In that sense it may even be said that, in the figures of Hermann and Segest, German and French culture meet and compete; but also that German national culture and cosmopolitanism clash as rivals. Between Hermann and Segest stands Flavius, the man of the divided heart and mind: It is his personal tragedy that he arrives too late at a true insight into the precious values which are at stake.

These then are the three stages of patriotism and inner independence as depicted in Schlegel's play: genuinely German—and mature—are the four figures of Sigmar, Adelheid, Hermann and Thusnelda. Hence they know no inner struggle. They are imperturbably German, i.e., anti-Roman (anti-French) and—quite like Klopstock! Vacillating for various reasons, though troubled by their consciences, are Flavius and Siegmund. Completely pro-"welsch" and, hence, lost to the German cause, are Segest and his group of unnamed followers. Though we are told that Segest, too, had once been a brave defender of his country's freedom, his basic selfishness has now won the upperhand. He has found his more expedient interests temporarily on the national rival's side: a victim of 'welsch' lures and lust of power, he thus turns traitor.

Flavius (Gottsched), on the other hand, hides his personal ambitions behind the argument of Roman cultural superiority. From her example Germany should learn and strive to tame her manners. Thus she should come to find herself and not lose her cultural identity. But Flavius also represents again the German sensitiveness to foreign slight and criticism: it hurts him to be looked upon as a German boor, to sense the foreigner's conceit, his haughty condescension and contempt.

Yet there can be no doubt about who wins out in the argument between father and son when Sigmar flatly warns his wavering second son: "rather free in our huts, than slaves in the palaces of Rome"[5]—rather dead than a slave! The entire play seems dedicated to bearing out this patriotic principle.

Between Schlegel's "Hermann" drama and Klopstock's "Hermann" trilogy stands a group of Arminius poets of minor rank, though all of them men of consequence at their own time. They furnished their patriotic contributions to the Arminius literature partly under Gottsched's aegis and partly under Klopstock's. They are Möser, von Schönaich, von Ayrenhoff, and Wieland.

Justus *Möser* (1720-'94) is better remembered to-day in the circles of jurists and historians than in the annals of literature. His "History of Osnabrück", of 1768, and his numerous small essays called "Patriotic Fantasies" (publ. since 1774) reveal him not only as an erudite historian and excellent prose stylist but also as a warm patriot with conservative, pedagogic leanings. To the student of Goethe, Möser remains of special interest as a contributor to a little volume published anonymously by Herder and Goethe, in 1773, under the title of "Concerning German Genius and Art" ('Von deutscher Art und Kunst'). Möser's contribution was taken from the introduction to his "History of Osnabrück." Here Möser, the anti-absolutist, extolled the ancient Teutonic spirit of freedom as a vanished ideal, while Herder sang the praises of German folk songs, demanding their collection and preservation. But Herder also praised Shakespeare and promised the coming of his German equal. Goethe, on the other hand, gave an enthusiastic account of the cathedral of Strassburg, extolling the Gothic as the one and truly German style.

Herder and Goethe were then both in their twenties while Möser was 53, a vigorous opponent of enlightened despotism with its bureaucracy. Still, he was a conservative and full of admiration for England and her constitution. He could not realize that he was contributing to a publication destined to become a kind of Manifesto for a new generation of German poets and young patriots in revolt who, under the spell of Klopstock and the leadership of this young Goethe, were soon to rejuvenate the German spirit. Under the banner of Rousseau, they challenged Voltaire, pitting nature against culture, feeling against reason, faith against doubt, and individual genius against artificial rules and obsolete tradition.

Möser's unpoetic "Arminius" tragedy was first published in 1749[6], nine years after Frederick the Great's accession to the throne of Prussia. The fruit of Möser's deep interest in Germanics, it also is a patriotic call for a strong prince who would unite all Germany. Thus it was meant to oppose German disunity and dispel the chronic spirit of particularism. Above all, it is a strong outcry "in tyrannos."

The editor of Möser's "Collected Works"[7] has excluded this "Arminius" play in alexandrine verse and only reprints the author's own introduction to its first edition.[8] Riffert[9] gives some excerpts from the rare book. He states that the play is "too reflective," that it "personifies principles" instead of giving genuine human characters, conflicts and emotions, and that his "Grossmut" kills this faultless hero in the end.

We do not hear that the play ever reached the stage, but it clearly reflects an ever-growing national consciousness and, with the rising star of Prussia, a new hope of German union.

In the instructive introduction to the play, the historian Möser speaks and takes issue with his main source, Tacitus. He holds that the Roman, for effective contrast, depicted the ancient Germans as unnecessarily primitive; that the long-established contacts between the two countries in many fields of culture—together with the long services of German nobles at Rome and in her legions—had long since brought about a much closer cultural similarity than is usually assumed. Möser then enters into a brief analysis of his chief characters, Arminius, Thusnelda, Sigest and Sigismund, whom—poetical wisdom permitting—he intends to present in his drama according to his above theory, though "toned down" in emotions. Only in his "zeal for the good, in accordance with the laws of prudence," was the hero to show real passion.

In Thusnelda the author admires above all the "beauty and propriety of her sex" as well as her heroic endurance in her sufferings brought about to such a large extent by her own father. This Sigest hates his country "because Arminius has set it free." Sigest has repeatedly betrayed Germany and her leader out of envy for the greater man, and "all this can only be atoned for in death." His son, Sigismund, on the other hand, is "at heart a loyal friend of Arminius" whom he admires sufficiently to forsake his Roman priesthood, though he remains torn between his father's evil schemes and the commands of his heart.

The rest of his figures, Möser assures us, are fictitious in character, even where he uses their historical names.

In brief, Möser follows Tacitus in his basic motifs but not in dramatic accent. He confines himself to the time *after* the Varus battle; he shuns, however, the immensely tragic possibilities within his hero which Tacitus had implied: the turn of the liberator of his people into an oppressor of his forcibly united nation with a possible revengeful turn against Rome herself. Möser's hero is almost too noble. His 'Grossmut' does become "the source of his (and the drama's) undoing" (V,5). But the modest author also tells us that he expects nothing from his hearers but to see in this drama a "dutiful contribution to common entertainment." He hopes it "will prove profitable to all"—in a moral as well as patriotic sense, no doubt, as the play preaches one nation, indivisible and happily united under one prince, wise, noble, forceful but law-abiding.

Christoph Otto, Baron von *Schönaich's* (1725-1807) heroic poem, "Hermann, or Germany Liberated," owes its short-lived significance in the history of German literature not so much to its own intrinsic merits—of which it harbors but few—as to the fact that its author, through Gottsched's indiscretion, became a victim of the famous Gottsched-Klopstock feud.

In 1750, Gottsched received an anonymous epic manuscript. His immediate reaction was one of genuine delight: he believed he had discovered the German poet who might be the answer to his prayers for a truly German national epic after his own heart, i.e., according to the rules of the ancients and—the French! Moreover, what a find in his campaign against the noisy triumphs of Klopstock's "Messiah!" He urged the author at once to enlarge his epopee from ten to twelve cantos. He had the book printed the following year with an elaborate dedication and introduction of his own and—by virtue of his office as literary dictator, and as dean of the philosophy faculty of Leipzig University—he imprudently crowned the unknown Baron, *in absentia*, as *poeta laureatus*. That was in 1752. With that the feud was on again. The Gottsched party cheered; the opponents jeered and ridiculed the innocent author and his work together with their real target, Professor Gottsched.

Thus it happens that the most important part of Schönaich's book, of 1751, is not the epopee itself but the introduction from the pen of Gottsched.[10] In fact, without the foreword to this little book our picture of Gottsched and his literary feuds might even be a shade less colorful. Here he not only gives us his aesthetic *credo* in a nutshell, he also reveals his aspirations for German literature when he states that "the essence of a national epic" seemed to him "*the assertion (Behauptung) of German honor towards foreigners*"; i.e., the scoring of successes in Germany's literary rivalry with France, from whom German poets must borrow the weapons for the contest. In this respect the Saxon Baron had proved his mettle. Gottsched did not let the occasion pass without shooting his arrows into the Klopstock camp, either by innuendo or by simply ignoring the name of the rhapsodic singer of the "Messiah" where, in all fairness, it should be mentioned. This Schönaich, however, "walks firmly in the footsteps of the greatest poets of antiquity and of the best among the modern," Gottsched rejoices. Then he compares the author's fable, his epic technique and his merits for national literature, most favorably to—Homer, Vergil, Tasso, and Voltaire's "Henriade," leaving the impartial reader wondering whether Gottsched could ever be so weak in judgment—or so blinded by personal aspirations and antipathies.

Speaking of the earlier Arminius literature, Gottsched surprises us by mentioning no one before Hagelgans (1643), Lohenstein, and Campistron; not even Hutten, Moscherosch and Rist. As to Johann Elias Schlegel, Gottsched now claims to have "guided" him in his Arminius undertaking! He also does not fail to mention his own efforts in giving Schönaich's masterpiece its final touches.

The most valuable part of the introduction, however, is Gottsched's theory on the essence of a perfect epopee which, to him, comes about perhaps once during a millenium. Here Homer and Vergil are Schönaich's great predecessors; the latter being Schönaich's direct example. If art, Gottsched argues, is the poetic imitation of nature, then the epopee is the imitation of one paramount heroic action. As such it is the crown of all poetic efforts. Not the hero himself or the story of his life are its subject, but the one heroic action in completion; in Schönaich's case the Varus battle, no more and no less.

Gottsched then differentiates between two types of epic fables, the pathetic and the moral type. In the former, passion ('Affekte') keeps the plot in motion; in the latter reason does this. In Homer's "Iliad" it is the wrath of Achilles ('Affekte'); in his "Odyssey" it is the unswerving determination of the hero to reach his realm, his wife and family (reason). Vergil, on the other hand, even succeeded in combining both these types in his masterpiece, where reason and passion take turns in moving the plot.

Gottsched holds that Schönaich created his "Hermann" epopee after the Vergilian model—and that he succeeded. For, here too, reason and passion move the plot in turns. In part I Hermann, who has returned from Rome, is sent by his father, Siegmar, on a mission to Marobod to win him as an ally against Rome. (Reason prevails—though it is always Siegmar who directs plans and action, and not the hero who gives his name to the story). On the way, and at Marobod's exotic court, which reminds the reader of Lohenstein's exoticism, adventures befall the hero (again quite in the Lohenstein manner) which upset and finally ruin his plans; Gismund, who is Marobod's chief adviser and a partisan of Rome, plots to have Hermann killed by his daughter, Mathilde. But the girl promptly falls in love with the charming stranger. She spares his life and quickly finds her death at her father's hand. Gismund then persuades Marbod to remain the balance of power between Germany and Rome in order to weaken and eventually ruin both: here passion moves the plot! Then Hermann returns home. He organizes the resistance against Rome among the allied tribes. He then begins the war which culminates in the defeat and death of Varus. Here reason and steadfast determination to save Germany from the Roman yoke move the action. Hence Gottsched believes to have proved his theory that both the pathetic *and* the moral type are skillfully employed in Schönaich's epic.

Moreover, even the unity of time is appropriately preserved: the "Iliad" plays over a period of about six weeks; the "Odyssey" over one to two months, whereas the "Aeneid" covers about six months. Schönaich's "Hermann" stands modestly in the middle, as it covers about 90 days, the Varus battle taking up the last three of them, as historically reported. Thus in this respect, too, Schönaich's epic proved quite satisfactory.

Comparing the respective purposes of his three master epics, Gottsched has this to say: the "Iliad" teaches that disunion among the leaders of a people will prove pernicious; their union, however, promotes the people's welfare. Vergil, on the other hand, teaches that the founder of a new realm must be god-fearing, kind-hearted and steadfast. The basic "moral" of Schönaich's "Hermann," however, has even two aspects: 1) that a truly patriotic, unselfish hero will be able to hold his own in battle against an enemy superior in power and strategy; 2) that a people unspoiled and accustomed to hardship will, in the end, prove superior in battle to a spoiled and degenerate nation. Hence, this national epic of Gottsched's choice even has a "double moral."

Gottsched's last point in his defense of this "Hermann" epic concerns the use of what he calls "machines"—"the deus ex machina" device, the use of apparitions and of allegorical figures such as "Discord" in Schönaich's case, after the model of the Greek goddess of strife, Eris. Homer employs these devices frequently, Vergil does so more sparingly. In the case of this "Hermann," it was difficult for the poet to avoid it, for color's sake. Lohenstein's profuse application of such devices is not even mentioned by Gottsched, but the use of allegories by Boileau and Voltaire justifies sufficiently Schönaich's procedure. Moreover, Schönaich showed his skill by using dreams for the appearances of Mannus, the eponym of the German race; and that of

Siegmar after his death in battle, in order to prophesy the impending victory. An analogous function is given to the old German soothsayer, Velleda. Although this Velleda is supposed to have lived at the end of the first Christian century, and not at the time of the Varus battle (9 A.D.), her presence is artistically justified by a similar application of poetic license in the case of Vergil's Dido.

Moreover, besides this compliance with established classical and modern patterns, Schönaich's "Hermann" has decided merits of its own, Gottsched assures us. Thus he mentions the author's "grace of expression", "the adaptation of his diction to respective circumstances", "the majestic and charming euphony ('Wohllaut') of the verse". In short, Gottsched finds ample cause to congratulate not only the author, but Germany upon her "first heroic poem which, according to the rules and patterns of the ancients, does deserve the name of an Epopee".

Yet later critics did not concur at all, despite Voltaire's perfunctory compliments in a letter to Gottsched[11]. The triumphant Leipzig professor must have sent Voltaire a translation, as the Frenchman mentions some corrections of mistakes in it.

Many comprehensive histories of German literature do not even mention Schönaich's name any more; for no one can doubt that, on that occasion, Gottsched had shot far beyond the mark. Yet, Schönaich's book has been reprinted several times and even was translated into French as late as 1799. Unfortunately, Gottsched's enthusiastic support proved doubly detrimental to Schönaich, who came to overrate his own literary talent. He ventured into drama and even took part in literary feuds on Gottsched's side; not only against the Klopstock party but even against the German master of 18th-century literary criticism, Lessing, who had ridiculed Schönaich's 'coronation' in literary reviews and possibly in one of his acid epigrams.

While it is true that Schönaich's "Hermann" is the first known German epic version of the Arminius theme, it is by no means a first-rate epic despite its "classic regularity" of which Gottsched made so much. The subject matter simply proved too much for Schönaich's sober and unpoetic mode of treatment. Even the trochaic meter proved uneven and quite tiresome. The main hero is but the doer of his father's bidding and still needs his guidance even after Siegmar's death. Siegmar and Hermann stand for union—they are patriots and, therefore, good. Marbod stands for division and, hence, is bad. Segest is again the traitor and, therefore, wicked. Varus is effeminate, haughty and weak and, hence, despicable. No doubt, Voltaire was right when he praised the "virtuous feelings" of the author. A warm patriot he was, indeed. But, as an artist, he pleads a bit too obviously in behalf of German unity and for a new national leadership under a new Arminius.

Cornelius von *Ayrenhoff* (1733-1819), Austrian general, German patriot and playwright, was by birth and breeding a child of the *ancien régime*. He witnessed the French Revolution, the Napoleonic cataclysm, and saw German classicism rise and wane. As a young officer he had participated in the Seven Years' War and later won high favor at the Viennese court. But his heart was with his country's enemy, the great king to the North, Frederick II, as his hopes were with a united Germany. His Jesuitic training had furnished the young nobleman with a thorough knowledge of the classics; yet his literary taste came to be French. As a partisan of Gottsched he therefore followed the French models and rejected Shakespeare.

It is true that Ayrenhoff was not a creative poet of rank. Yet he occupies a leading place in the protracted struggle for a modern German stage and also exerted a strong influence during his long lifetime as one of the great German national patriots. His plays, too, serve a double purpose, one cultural and artistic and the other patriotic. From the fraticidal contest between Austria and Prussia for hegemony in the heart of Europe, Ayrenhoff, together with some of the best men of his time, derived the vision of German cultural integration with political union as its ultimate goal. With Elias Schlegel, Lessing, and Klopstock, Ayrenhoff shares his efforts for a German national drama; with Möser he holds his high political hopes in common[12]. They both are, moreover, imbued with the Prussian king's stern ethos of the individual's duty towards his state or nation, and the shadow of that stoic 'first servant' of his rising state falls squarely across the Arminius world of the patriotic Austrian playwright. So do the shadows of Klopstock and Rousseau. Moreover, the ultimate purpose of Ayrenhoff's 'Arminius' is war upon any kind of tyranny and despotism on this earth:

- - - - - Ich will die Tyrannei

In dem verhassten Blut des letzten Römers strafen;
Ich will *der ganzen Welt* Recht, Glück und Rache schaffen[13].

Thus the Cheruscan tribal leader is elevated to the state of an illustrious national hero; but he also is offered to an abused humanity as *the* protagonist of justice and freedom—sources of true human happiness.

In an appendix to his first Arminius drama the author states his purpose directly: "to acquaint the nation better with *her greatest hero* and, through the deeds of her forefathers, to kindle within her soul the fires of fortitude and of an *extinguished patriotism*".

That von Ayrenhoff's generation still offered cause for such concern and criticism is brought out by a passing glance at the cosmopolitan Lessing's political *credo*. In his correspondence Lessing[14] once remarked that "the reputation of a patriot would be the last thing I should strive for; i.e., a patriotism which would make me forget that I am, above all else, a citizen of the world" (Weltbürger). Then again the writer refers to the love of one's country as "a heroic weakness which I can gladly do without"[15].

The gulf between Elias Schlegel, Möser, Ayrenhoff, the Klopstock circle—together with the patriotic poets about the victorious Frederick—on the one hand, and the unpolitical, humanitarian cosmopolitanism which prevailed among the rising German classicists, was indeed profound. While most of the German populace rarely glanced beyond their little states and local regions, it was the meteoric rise of Prussia which quickly kindled a new patriotic zeal in the hearts of the admirers of the successful Prussian king. Just as later, during the days before the Wars of Liberation from Napoleon, so the patriots from the four corners of Germany—with intellectuals and artists in the lead—now rallied to the standards of the expanding northern state as the only promise of a united German nation of the future.

Ayrenhoff's dramatic activities are closely linked with the history of the famous Burgtheater of Vienna and with its gradual emancipation from the long-prevailing French-Italian repertoire and taste[16]. Before the appearance of Goethe's "Goetz," in 1773, Ayrenhoff had already produced for the German stage five plays which enjoyed immediate and wide popularity all over Austria and Germany. This success holds true especially of his comedies. One of them, "Der Postzug" (1769) won the special favor of the Prussian king and was performed at Berlin not less than forty times within ten years. The author states that it was his endeavor to replace the old-type burlesque, which had developed out of the *commedia dell' arte*, by a worthier type of German comedy. His zeal for a higher moral level of the stage inspired the young author from the start. We find it also expressed in his various aesthetic writings. Between the years 1766 and 1775, Ayrenhoff contributed to the bills of the Burgtheater four tragedies and three comedies. The next year, 1776, saw the end of the old-type burlesque on that stage and its elevation to the rank of 'Hof-und Nationaltheater.' Since 1754 it had eked out a precarious financial existence under the high-sounding name of 'Théatre français près de la cour' when Italian and French ballets, operas and plays had been the vogue among social circles, while the older Kärntnerthor Theater had flourished with its homespun and trivial burlesques. Since the 1780s, Lessing's, Schiller's and Goethe's plays, together with Mozart operas, appear on the Burgtheater programs. Yet it is indicative of the temper of that ultra-conservative court that plays with the slightest revolutionary tinge—such as young Schiller's "The Robbers," "Don Carlos," "Cabal and Love," and also Goethe's "Goetz," were kept off the stage until 1807. Ayrenhoff may have had a hand in this circumspect censorship, for his dislike for such works, as those of Shakespeare and the young patriotic rebels of the 'Storm and Stress' movement—enthusiastic followers of Klopstock and Rousseau—was quite pronounced.

Yet Ayrenhoff was far from ever rejecting Italian and French art. He knew those languages and their literatures and delighted in their operas and plays. But the stage of his day was to him a means to an end: the education of the people, the moral improvement and nationalization of the German mind. Good German dramas still were rare. When the last French group left the Burgtheater, in 1772, and ballet and opera were discontinued, there must have been a constant demand for new material. Thus Ayrenhoff took to the pen in a sense of patriotic duty.

His first tragedy, "Aurelius," in alexandrine verse, was first performed in 1766. It was published in a revised version in 1768 and reveals its author not only as a rationalist who warns of the dangers of uncontrolled passion but also as a character of lofty moral principles. The fable is the author's free invention.

His hero's sublime character triumphs over his rebellious foes—an enviable fate which this author's equally magnanimous Arminius figure, unfortunately, does not share; for Arminius becomes the victim of his own nobility of soul.

Ayrenhoff gives us his dramatic principle: the stirring of violent passions as the *a priori* condition of the tragic poet's plot. To this the playwright has adhered throughout his dramatic career. But patriotism and the wish to present a strong political moral led him to Arminius, in whom he saw 'Germany's first *national* hero.' Thus Ayrenhoff too equates the 'Germania prisca' with the 'Germania recentior,' as the humanists had done before.

The Austrian playwright even wrote two Arminius plays. The first one, a tragedy in alexandrine verse, appeared in 1768 under the title of "Hermann und Thusnelda". It was revised at once and reprinted under the new title of "Hermann's Tod," in 1769. Hermann's son, Thumelicus, is the main hero of the second drama which appeared in 1770, first as "Thumelicus, or Hermann Avenged," later on, in the Collected Works, which went through five editions between 1772 and 1817, it bore the name of "Hermanns Rache" (Hermann's Revenge).

"Hermann's Death" is written in the Gottschedian vein. Though its author knew his Tacitus and was well acquainted with Lohenstein's 'Arminius,' he must have been inspired mainly by Möser, Schönaich and Schlegel; perhaps also by young Wieland's epic 'Hermann' fragment.

It seems that Schlegel's drama influenced Ayrenhoff most, for his own "Hermann's Death" is, so to speak, a continuation of Schlegel's play. While Schlegel had depicted the Varus battle and the liberation of Germany, Ayrenhoff opens his drama with the subsequent quarrel among the German leaders. Thusnelda and Thumelicus are being returned from captivity by a Roman officer, Sejanus, and are offered to Arminius in exchange for a treaty of peace. The Germans prefer to refuse as they wish to continue the war to the point of a complete Roman defeat. Thus Hermann is faced with a terrible decision: to sacrifice Thusnelda and his own son in the interest of his country and, perhaps, lose both for ever—or to buy an uneasy, temporary peace and forsake his own mission as the national liberator of an imperiled Germany. Again, as in Schlegel's version, we encounter Schiller's later, favorite theme of the conflict between duty and inclination.

Here political duty towards one's people is in conflict with the hero's personal love. Thusnelda's magnanimous self-sacrifice as she offers to return voluntarily to Rome equals Hermann's own stoutness of heart. While Segestes, enraged over Hermann's unselfish decision, openly threatens to rejoin the Roman side and is promptly taken prisoner, Hermann offers him his hand as a token of friendship and reconciliation. At once Segestes draws his dagger and stabs his noble-hearted son-in-law. Hermann dies in Thusnelda's arms. She, in turn, kills herself over the body of Arminius.

That, in brief outline, is the story of the tragic end of the great Cheruscan as interpreted by Ayrenhoff.

Riffert[17] terms the drama a failure because of "the total absence of tragic guilt on the part of the hero" who perishes as the victim of purely personal hate while Germany's fate is left hanging in the balance. The wrath of Segestes, which leads to the revolt in which this traitor, too, finally perishes is based on errors, intrigues (Adgandester-Sejanus) and misunderstanding. Those can be basic shortcomings in a tragedy, no doubt. Yet it can not be denied that the play exerts a powerful effect and its final appeal for German harmony and union did not go unheeded. The success of its *première* at Vienna, we are told, was overwhelming. Hermann's message as the finale of the play,

"Denn Zwietracht ist der Deutschen ärgster Feind"[18],

is a worthy counterpart to the dying Attinghausen's plea in Schiller's "Wilhelm Tell," 'Seid einig, einig, einig.' Ayrenhoff's "Arminius" reveals its author as a high-minded and courageous national patriot in a thoroughly unpatriotic age.

The fable of "Thumelicus, or Hermann's Revenge," a tragedy in 36 scenes with chorus, is largely the author's free invention, though it probably was suggested by some remarks of Tacitus concerning the later career of Italus, son of Flavius, in Germany. The play shows the influence of Klopstock's "Hermanns Schlacht", in structure as well as in the use of the bardic chorus.

Thumelicus and his Roman wife Aelia, daughter of Sejanus, have returned from Rome, and Thumelicus is promptly chosen as the Cheruscan leader. But an oracle demands that Hermann's blood must be avenged. Velleda, a prophetess, points at Aelia, as Sejanus, her father, had been involved in Hermann's death. At the last moment the error in the interpretation of the oracle is cleared up. Aelia is saved by Thumelicus from her unjust fate and Adgandester, surviving instigator of the intrigue against Hermann, is put to death instead.

This drama is the weaker of the two. In some respects, it anticipates the technique of the later fate tragedies. Its figures lack in individuality, while the action is moved largely by errors which are, in turn, cleared up by chance, and just before it is too late. Learned, mythological elements impede the understanding of the lengthy bardic songs which recite history and show scant relation to the dramatic plot.

We are told that the play was performed twice, in Vienna, with the Klopstock-inspired chorus appropriately left out.

While Schönaich was writing his 'Hermann' epic (in 1751), young Christoph Martin *Wieland* (1733-1813), then a student at Tübingen University, likewise engaged in plans for a 'Hermann' epic. Neither knew of the other. Schönaich addressed his completed work anonymously to his idol, Gottsched. Wieland, then an ardent admirer of the seraphic singer, Klopstock, turned— and equally anonymously—with his first epic fragment to the Swiss, Bodmer. The famous Zürich critic was at that time an enthusiastic protagonist of the young author of the "Messiah." Prompted by Bodmer, and in a spirit of criticism of Schönaich's weak epic production, Wieland continued for a while and enlarged upon his early sketch. Yet he quickly outgrew his halfhearted enthusiasm for the world of the bards, for shadowy Germanic heroes and Teutonic mythology, whither his devotion to Klopstock had misled him. His interest soon lagged entirely in spite of Bodmer's encouraging praise, and in spite of the appearance of the first fragments of his "Hermann" in the Zürich 'Freimütigen Nachrichten,' of December 1751. But in Bodmer the young poet had won an intimate friend and a *pater confessor* for the most formative years of his life. Another brief section of the epic appeared in 1755. This was meant as a direct challenge to his rival in the Gottsched camp, Schönaich, and bore the title of "From the Improved Hermann." Wieland's entire "Hermann" manuscript was not published until 1882.[19] It had been left out of the earlier editions of Wieland's Works, as the author had rejected it in later years. This final version of Wieland's "Hermann" epic consists of four cantos in hexameters.

While Riffert[20] still passes it by, P. von Hofmann-Wellenhof[21], who knew the Muncker edition of the epic, takes issue with Wieland's fragment. Hofmann sees in Wieland's 'Hermann' version not so much an attempt to extol the early Cheruscan but, rather, an anticipatory version of one of Wieland's later favorite themes: the triumph of virtue over all temptations and tribulations. It is precisely this theme of *'sophrosyne'* gained from a hard-won conquest of self which links this 'Hermann'—and Wieland's later mental world—to the world of Lohenstein's magnanimous Arminius, who was young Wieland's major source. Beside this motif of the individual's struggle with his self, Wieland's exhortations of his countrymen, to follow in patriotic zeal and sacrifice in the footsteps of their heroes from a worthier past, sound fairly hollow and rhetorical. Hofmann emphasizes further the fact that, compared with the majority of the Arminius presentations of the sixteenth and seventeenth centuries where women—even Thusnelda herself, if she appears at all—played but minor rôles, the relationship between Hermann and Thusnelda comes more and more to the fore and soon becomes a major theme. In this respect, too, Wieland shares Lohenstein's psychological curiosity: his interest in the personal struggles which permeate and complicate the major political story from their psychic and individual angle. Thus Wieland's 'Hermann' version too accentuates again the tragic love story paralleled by others (Flavius and Catta); and the immoral deportment of the lascivious Varus is, as with Lohenstein, made into the main cause of the revolt. In this manner the day of the Varus battle—with the death of the unworthy Roman noble at the hands of his enraged German foe—becomes not only the 'bringer of freedom,' but also signifies the 'doom of vice' and the 'sacred avenger of innocence.' Hence young Wieland gives us, instead of the outlines of a national epopee, all the elements of a rather individualized drama in which personal virtues triumph while vice and evil stand exposed and judged. Thus even the young Wieland stands much closer to the baroque world of a Lohenstein, and to the mental climate of Rococo and Enlightenment, than to the world of his patriotic contemporaries gathered about Klopstock and the Prussian king. Little did Wieland realize even in retrospect, that—despite its shortcomings—his 'Hermann' fragment would prove his own superiority as an epic poet—not only when compared to his source, Lohenstein, and to the Gottsched pupil Schönaich, but even when likened to his revered prototype and singer of the lofty "Messiah," Klopstock.

Friedrich Gottlieb *Klopstock* (1724-1803) is modern Germany's first inspired seer-poet: a passionate singer of religion, of nature as God's creation, of mother-tongue, love, fatherland and friendship in a world where Reason and Rococo seem to rule supreme. These concepts fill and circumscribe his mental world. To them and, thence, to German poetry Klopstock has lent a pristine depth and well-nigh sacred dignity unheard-of by the German ear since Luther's day. For with Klopstock, too, the well-spring of every psychic experience is his religion. He and Herder, above all others, have filled the terms of 'Volk,' 'Volkstum,' 'Deutschtum,' 'Nation,' and 'Vaterland' with a new and mystic element, thus giving them an almost virgin ring. This emotional factor is difficult for the non-German to grasp. Yet to do so seems of paramount importance for the understanding of the modern German's peculiar psychic responses to his political experiences and dreams. Its grasp is made doubly difficult since those terms and their manifold interrelations have undergone considerable changes during the course of Germany's troubled history.

Furthermore, Klopstock's personal patriotism has had a far-reaching effect on the growth of German national consciousness. The exalted singer of the miracles of creation and salvation is equally awe-struck by the mystery of the *logos* through which Man's mind, and the poet's mind above all others, becomes creative. Its miracle works at the root of all things that make for human understanding, hence also for those sacred bonds of cultural communities called nations. And Lincoln's lofty proposition "that this nation, under God, shall have a new birth of freedom" was just as firmly embedded in Klopstock's heart.

At the occasion of the bicentennial of the poet's birth, in 1924, a medal was struck which bears two significant inscriptions. They justly extol Klopstock as the poet of religion and of patriotism. On the one side stands engraved the opening line from his 'Messiah',

Sing, unsterbliche Muse, der sündigen Menschen Erlösung.[22]

On the other side an equally revealing quotation from one of Klopstock's patriotic odes is to be found,

Ich sinne dem edlen, schreckenden Gedanken nach,
Deiner wert zu sein, mein Vaterland.[23]

Such patriotism is indeed not political and far from being chauvinistic; it is religiously inspired, highly idealistic and humane.

Klopstock's own contributions to the Arminius literature are but part of his far-flung patriotic poetry. They consist of a number of odes and a cycle of three Hermann plays, called *Bardiete*. These are not meant to be dramas in the customary sense but series of dramatic scenes with bardic song-interludes; i.e., free versions of the Arminius story told in the alleged style of Celtic bards. They were written for a young generation. Yet, whatever their historic misconceptions and dramatic failings may be—for Klopstock was a 'naive' poet and a lyrical genius who lacked the dramatist's and scholar's objectivity—it can not be denied that the poet's own enthusiasm for Germanic antiquity, which embraced his heroes Arminius and Thusnelda, inflamed a young generation to new heights of patriotic fervor. It also stimulated a new interest in a scholarly approach to Germanic history and philology such as only the humanists had known before—thus checking, or at least counteracting, the high tide of cosmopolitanism prevalent in this age.

On the other hand, it was not Klopstock's fault if he helped to unleash that vogue of insipid 'Bardengeheul' (bardic howling) which soon swept Germany from the North Sea to the Danube and the Alps, and against which Klopstock's own good taste protested, just as he abhorred all mental mediocrity and irreverence. Its appearance rather reflects the ever-growing tide of patriotic protest against the triumphs of that a-patriotic cosmopolitanism. The excesses on the part of his imitators were the penalty the poet had to pay for his far-reaching popularization of the Germanic past. And had not the spell of the recently discovered, though fictitious Celtic bard, Ossian, gripped the singer of the "Messiah" himself?

Conversely, it can not be denied that it was Klopstock who raised the standards of 'Virtue, Freedom, Fatherland' to unprecedented heights when, in the face of foreign taste and fashion, he preached that the patriotic virtues must be counted among the foremost moral virtues. He did so by force of his inimitable poetic diction and an ever-youthful and idealistic fervor, though he was unable to prevent his lofty patriotism from being at times degraded into a heated Germanomania among Philistine circles. In that he shared the fate of many a lofty idealist of the ages.

From his youth Klopstock had been an individualist, proud and eager for personal success. In the highly competitive atmosphere of the famous Pforta School, where the classics ruled and whence Schlegel had just made his way to literary fame, Klopstock had discovered that the Muses had favored him too with poetic imagination and the magic of words. This mastery over others he exercised with skill and zest, but ever-conscious of his responsibility and lofty mission. Inspired by Milton and the classics, the youth set out to sketch his "Messiah". The appearance of its first three cantos, in 1748, fulfilled his dreams beyond all expectations: it made him famous at the age of twenty-four. And justly so, for his work marked the end of the French-inspired German neo-classicism and opened a new era of great German literature. He had set out to give his Germans their first national epic and, in keeping with his pietistic leanings, on a religious basis; and he did it two years before his literary antagonist, Gottsched, took occasion to claim this honor for the mediocre work of Schönaich.

Young Klopstock's patriotic enthusiasm had been centered upon the early Saxon king, Henry I, victor over the Magyars in the famous Lechfeld battle in the vicinity of Augsburg in 955. This Henry, too, had been a liberator from impending foreign conquest and tyranny. But from 1752 on—and under the influence of Schlegel and later perhaps also of Wieland—the poet's patriotic interest turns to the figure of Arminius. His enthusiasm for the Cheruscan was to accompany him through the major part of his poetic career. For the last ode glorifying Hermann dates from 1794; forty years after the first ode, called "Hermann und Thusnelda." Into about the middle of this long period fall the first two dramas of the trilogy, "Hermanns Schlacht," of 1767 (printed in 1769), and "Hermann und die Fürsten," of 1767/8 (not published until 1784). The third and last play, "Hermanns Tod", originated between 1785 and 1787.

It has been asserted[24] that Klopstock's image of Arminius is an idealized composite of the poet's impressions of the Prussian king, Frederick II, and of his one-time host and Maecenas, king

Frederick V of Denmark, who had made the young private tutor independent for his great literary career.

That those two men have colored Klopstock's Arminius picture is beyond all doubt, for they were perhaps the two outstanding public figures of his time who strongly influenced the poet's inner life. Yet Klopstock's relations to the Prussian monarch were somewhat of the Wagner-Nietzsche type: a peculiar blend of fascination, admiration, devotion, revolt and aversion. Whereas, in the person of the Danish king, Klopstock extolled the Christian prince of peace, the guardian of the arts, of culture and humaneness, in the Prussian ruler he hated the skeptic, the religious agnostic, the gross conqueror; but, above all, the scoffer at his native tongue and culture. Conversely, while strongly rejecting all wars of aggression—which needs breed a spirit of hate and revenge—Klopstock is fascinated by the superb generalship and stoic heroism of the victorious prince who seemed to exemplify the soldierly virtues at their very best. For these virtues are of equal significance for the only justifiable and glorious war—the war of defense and for freedom. In this light, the poet's enthusiasm for the American Revolution, as for the initial stages of the French, stand out: they both are, to him, justified and almost sacred wars upon an intolerably despotic system.

Klopstock's daring attitude towards the Prussian ruler—doubly bold in that servile age—has found vivid expression in a number of odes in which the poet at once lauds and then again castigates the 'un-German' soldier-king. However, to Klopstock this is not presumptuous at all but the sacred office of the seer-poet. He must speak out, accuse and censure; for he, too, is a defender of his country's honor, a guardian of its freedom and its virtues.

In an ode, "Die Rache" (Revenge) written in 1772, Klopstock chastizes the king for despising his sacred mother-tongue and his country's culture. He calls him a 'Fremdling im Heimischen' (a foreigner in his native element), an 'Ungeweihten in der Sprache Geheimnis' (one uninitiated into the mystery of his native tongue). Here, Klopstock holds, the soldierly hero has turned traitor to his nation. Pride in his country bids the prophet-poet break through all bonds of modesty and become his people's wrathful avenger.

Earlier, in 1768, Klopstock, in an ode "Mein Vaterland," had depicted his country as he wished it to be. Here he speaks of the two poles of his poetic mission, God and country, calling God's heavens 'das Vaterland des Menschengeschlechts'—mankind's fatherland. He leaves no doubt that glorifying God and His creation (work on the "Messiah") is his foremost poetic calling. Only when this awesome burden strains his human strength beyond endurance, does he exchange the harp for the Telyn[25]—the praise of the Lord for the praise of his earthly home. Then the poet celebrates the greatness of the ancient Germans, who have colonized Gaul and Britain and even have bestowed their German names on them[26]. But above all, they have broken the yoke of the 'Welttyrannin' Rome, thus establishing Germany's glory for the ages. He then turns to the character traits of Germany, such as he sees them through the course of history,

Nie war, gegen das Ausland,
Ein anderes Land gerecht, wie du!
Sei nicht allzugerecht. Sie denken nicht edel genug,
Zu sehen, wie schön dein Fehler ist- -[27]

And he continues,

Einfältiger Sitte bist du, und weise,
Bist ernsteren, tieferen Geistes, Kraft ist dein Wort,
Entscheidung dein Schwert. Doch wandelst du's gern
  in die Sichel, und triefst,
Wohl dir! von dem Blute nicht der anderen Welten![28]

Hence, his ideal nation appears to this poet as one mighty in the defence of her liberty; but tolerant, fair even to the point of weakness, towards other peoples. Above all, unjust wars are foreign to her since she loves a just and honorable peace.

Those are the noble qualities of Klopstock's Arminius too. In an ode, called "Hermann," of the year 1767, we find the essence of the later trilogy anticipated. The ode is supposed to be sung by three bards who, on the day of the hero's funeral, mourn Arminius' unjust death. 'His country's noblest son', he is called. He who was 'Rome's secret terror' has been laid low by their country's traitors (Segestes, Adgandester, etc.). But the victor over Varus is called the 'darling of the noblest', the 'leader of the boldest' and, above all, the 'liberator of his fatherland'. From this ode we also learn the secret aspirations of this faultless hero: not only did he plan more victories over the Roman legions in Germany—if the jealous German princes (the selfish particularists) had not interfered, Hermann surely would have sent Caecina the way of Varus. This Hermann did plan the march on Italy and Rome—in contrast to all historical sources which only record the fear of it which gripped Rome after Varus' débâcle. To achieve his end, Klopstock's Hermann strives for the German 'generalship' (das Feldherrnschwert); but only for the time of the war alliance against Rome, and never for a German kingship of his own:

'- - To *die* there (in Rome)! *or* in the proud Capitol, near the scales of Jove, to question Tiberius and his sires' shades about the *justice* of their wars! *To do so he strove to carry the general's sword* among the princes - -'

Such, then, is this Arminius' lofty purpose: to wipe out age-old injustice inflicted upon his innocent people by Rome; to avenge German blood and honor at the very 'scales of Jove'; but

"- - da zückten sie den Tod auf ihn!
Und im Blute liegt nun der, in dessen Seele war
Der grosse Vaterlandsgedanke."[29]

'Der grosse Vaterlandsgedanke'—hub of Klopstock's mental world on earth—where did it burn purer at his time, though still as a phantom-dream, alas, but in this poet's and his Hermann's noble heart?: God, humanity, and a nation resplendent with the virtues of honor, love of liberty and justice. Only his innocent paganism could possibly separate his Arminius from this Christian poet's vision of German excellence; this poet whose true home would be—if not among the seraphim—at least an ideal, though aristocratic republic made up of well-nigh perfect beings and zealous patriots. Thus his Arminius obviously reflects not only Klopstock's vision of the ideal patriot and statesman, but also his ideal man. But will he be a truly tragic hero on the stage as well?

In a letter to emperor Joseph II[30], to whom the "Hermanns Schlacht" is dedicated, Klopstock states, "my mind is directed towards the noble and great". This certainly holds true for his Hermann dramas, too; for the exalted and heroic are this poet's elements by birth-right. Ethically speaking, these dramas are worthy counterparts to Schiller's "Wilhelm Tell" and to Hölderlin's incomparable song of Athens' fight for freedom, "Der Archipelagus": *dulce et decorum est pro patria mori*! All these are inspired works. They aim to instill into a new generation a new sense of duty and self-sacrifice towards their imperiled country. In that respect the Druids and Bards, who accompany the action in Klopstock's play with their rituals and songs that seek to arouse and inspire the warriors before and during battle, are actually among the leading figures; while Siegmar, venerable and aging father of the youthful German leader, sets a glorious example as he crowns a long and useful life with his voluntary death in the battle for freedom.

Klopstock's *"Hermanns Schlacht,"* a 'bardiet' in 14 scenes, describes the third and final day of the decisive Varus battle. The locale is a broad rock overlooking the valley where the battle is fought. There are but seven major persons in the play, besides the priestly Druids and the singing bards. They are Hermann and his parents, Siegmar and Bercennis, plus their wayward son, Flavius; then Segestes with his children, Siegmund and Thusnelda. The ideal of the stalwart patriots among them is Brutus, not Caesar. The best figure in the play is old Siegmar, who represents a life of unselfish devotion to the highest patriotic ideals, beloved and revered by all.

It may be observed that the wild ferocity of Lohenstein's German warriors in battle has been considerably toned down by Klopstock. The course of the battle itself is reported by messengers and observers from vantage points. The uncertainty of battle, together with occasional rumors concerning the fate of Siegmar and Hermann, furnish the only elements of tension throughout these picture-scenes. Approximately one third of the time is taken up by the bardic chorus which sings of past heroic deeds, occasionally following such praises by Roman writers.

One such chorus stands out for its remarkably effective simplicity as it extols the strength of the united nation,
    Du gleichst der dicksten, schattigsten Eiche
    Im innersten Hain,
    Der höchsten, ältesten, heiligsten Eiche,
    O Vaterland[31].

The prevalence of the chorus reflects this play's melodramatic character, but also its basic dramatic weakness. Yet there are occasional traits of human relationship which lift some scenes to a high level of dramatic effect and beauty.

Among the leading male figures besides Siegmar is Brenno, the druidic high priest. He and Siegmar are the wise counselors and moral judges by virtue of their age, wisdom and public stature. Their praise is high reward, their decisions are fair and final. Before this Brenno the traitors Segest, Siegmund, and Flavius are brought in turn and hear their judgment. Before him, Siegmund is won back to his country's cause. But the priest's stern verdict—as again when Flavius appears before him in chains—is tempered with clemency at the intercession of the noble-hearted and compassionate Thusnelda. Through this Druid's mouth we hear the poet moralize. When the treacherous Segest makes an attempt to justify his pro-Roman stand, the priest sends him back to his Roman friends in disgrace by stating bluntly, "Your people choose freedom, and you crave bondage" (Scene 4). And again, in Scene 11, when Brenno reproaches the haughty Roman captive, Valerius, as follows, "Injustice is the pillar of your (Roman) greatness. The storm of the gods will tumble its rocky structure—and the storm may come from the North" (i.e., from Germany); to which Hermann himself adds this, "You *appear* to be just; I *am*, and want to be so." Moreover, the return of the Roman priest, Siegmund, to his people's side during the course of the battle—his test and re-acceptance at the hands of the patriotic priest—is one of the most moving scenes of the play. Another dramatic climax is achieved in the same scene (6) when the youths attending the altar of the high priest, inspired by the chorus and by Siegmund's return, crave Brenno's permission to rush into battle and help stem the tide of the hard-pressing foe. The scene is followed by the heroic death of the brave young son of Werdomar, leader of the bards.

However, in the presentation of some other human relationships the play seems to be wanting.

The scene of Arminius-Thusnelda as they meet after victory, lacks warmth—the hero supposedly being too occupied with the aftermath of battle to respond freely to her jubilant approach. In this respect, the ode of 1752[32], which takes up the same dramatic moment, is far superior in poetic effect. Moreover, the Hermann-and-his-mother relation is marred by the harsh attitude of Bercennis as she demands death for all Roman captives in revenge for her husband's death in battle. That these hard features are perhaps meant to put Hermann's own noble humaneness into its proper perspective, can hardly reconcile the hearer when, to his mother's blunt reproach, "You refuse revenge," the hero retorts, "No, but only on the living legions"; i.e., in battle with Rome's future armies in the field (Scene 14).

A general oath of future revenge for Siegmar's death is then proclaimed by Werdomar, the bard, which concludes the first play of the trilogy on a heroic note.

This first 'bardiet' was meant to extol the heroic exploits of the German warrior and the strength of German unity in action, with the Varus battle as the paramount event in early German history. The 'bardiet' as a poetic form was something new in literature. Its first reception was enthusiastic. It inspired poets of all ranks, and the musicians too. Yet, despite all efforts on the part of various stage directors—Klopstock himself wished to see the plays performed in the open—little ever came of it. It seems the entire trilogy has never been performed. The effective beauty of individual scenes could not make up for the inherent dramatic weakness of the whole; and naturally so: a 'bardiet' for the stage is a contradiction in itself.

In the specific case of "Hermanns Schlacht", there are but two figures of convincing stature, Siegmar and Brenno, the Druid. The others, even Hermann himself, are a bit unbending. At times, their actions remain unmotivated. Here, too, the figures are divided too sternly into the good and the bad; i.e., the patriotic and, hence, noble-minded, and the unpatriotic ones, the weak or wicked; with the Romans as the haughty representatives of a violent, unjust tyranny.

Brenno is the representative of justice. 'Justice is mild,' he exclaims. Thusnelda, on the other hand, represents compassion and a spirit of forgiveness. But she knows no psychic conflicts over her dual loyalty to a wicked parent and her hero-husband. Hermann shows the traits of both, Brenno and Thusnelda, as the occasion warrants it. He lacks convincing naturalness, and the title of the play might just as well be 'Siegmar.'

"*Hermann und die Fürsten*" (Hermann and the Princes), on the other hand, offers far better pictures of human passion and of psychological motivations. While the first 'bardiet' is mainly heroic in nature, as it depicts Germany's invincibility when united—though the defection of Segest and Flavius foreshadows the tragic mood of the later plays—"Hermann und die Fürsten" is full of human pathos. It portrays the hero's tragic inner isolation and his sufferings—the price of greatness—in view of the irreconcilable jealousy and suspicions on the part of his political antagonists. In short, Germany's age-old weakness, inner discord and the dangers of selfish particularism, are its major theme.

Seven years have elapsed since Hermann's victory over Varus, and Roman legions are again in Northern Germany. Segest and his fickle son, Siegmund, have joined the Roman side once more. Thusnelda and her oldest son, Thumelicus, are in enemy hands, thanks to Segest's evil machinations.

Another decisive battle is at hand. Two days of fighting under Hermann's leadership have proved successful, but that is all his rivals for the glory can endure. Now Hermann urges them to lure the Romans from their camp into swamps and woods and deal them a final blow. All portents are for victory. Yet Hermann's opponents insist on storming the Roman camp instead—an obvious strategic risk, and Hermann warns against it.

As the play opens we behold the German princes in council, with Hermann temporarily absent. The atmosphere is charged with antipathy. Hate and envy of the hero's fame are in the air. Indeed, throughout most of the play's 16 scenes, Hermann has to grapple with this shadowy monster of unfounded suspicion and petty obstinacy. Thus, at the climax of his undeserved anguish we hear him exclaim, "Ye gods, spare me this one misery that I have to despair of my fatherland!" For his obvious tragedy is this: his one chance to defeat the foe decisively is at hand—but he is forced to let it go while a handful of petty rivals threaten to plunge them all into an almost catastrophic defeat.

Thus the major figures of the play (about sixteen) are divided into the pro- and contra-Hermann factions, besides a few wavering ones and the open traitors. Behind Hermann stands, above all, Brenno, the aged, half-blind, and venerable Druid priest; then youthful and valiant Katwald, a radiant Siegfried nature and closest to the hero's heart. Katwald's older brother, Malvend[33], is the leader of the Marsi; Arpe is prince of the Catti. He is, at present, accompanied by his patriotic wife and daughter, Istaewona and Herminone, both staunch admirers of their hero, Hermann. Ingomar, on the other hand, leads the anti-Hermann forces. He is the hero's uncle and present ruler over the Cheruscans. As with Tacitus' Inguiomerus, he opposes Hermann because honor forbids him to submit to the counsel and leadership of the younger, though abler man. There is, moreover, Gambriv, obstinate leader of the Bructi tribe. The latter two, above all others, 'do not hear the voice of reason.' It even becomes obvious that most of these princes would rather accept defeat at the hands of the common foe than grant Hermann the glory of another Roman victory. Therein lies the irony of this second play. Ingomar even hides his selfish aims behind the democratic principle of rule and decision by majority while hoping to sway a sufficient number of the princes against their chosen leader. "Are you not the leader?" the astonished Druid priest asks of Hermann; whereupon Gambriv retorts, "The princes are the leader, Druid!"; then Brenno again: "and Caecina the victor!"

In the utterances of this wise warner and fearless priestly prophet—apparently the only one who dares speak the truth at all times—one believes one feels the very heart-pulse of the drama. For Brenno accompanies its action like a Greek chorus and thus occupies again a key position. His relation to Hermann (one of the finest features of this play) is that of a fatherly friend who comforts and counsels the suffering ones; who rebukes selfishness and treason; who encourages and praises brave deeds. It is Brenno who castigates Flavius for his shameful disloyalty when this renegade German makes his shameless appearance as a messenger of Caecina (Scene 6)[34]; while his unspoiled little son, Italus, tries so manfully to coax his father back to the German side. It is Brenno again who turns his face from the wounded Ingomar in stern rebuke, "You have robbed your country of a second Varus battle and have led it to the brink of destruction" (Scene 14). And finally, it is this Brenno who—though he is now in chains and Hermann has fled—proudly utters these prophetic words in the face of his amazed Roman captors, "You may beat us in battle, but you shall never conquer Germany!" which brings this play to its climactic conclusion and reminds one again of Tacitus' "proeliis victus—bello non victus."

Though this second 'bardiet' is indeed a tragic picture of human selfishness and frailty against which no greatness of soul nor personal heroism prevails, the drama also possesses some noble human traits. These are embodied not only in the hero himself and in the noble priest—but especially in the figures of the brave and unspoiled youths, Theude, Hermann's second son, and Italus, his nephew, in whom 'the voice of nature' speaks, though he knows only Rome. But these traits are also manifested in the fearless figure of Katwald who, despite his youth, has this to say to the quarrelsome princes (Scene 1), "Out of envy you misjudge Hermann, the liberator of our country"; while, shortly before the end, he admonishes Theude, "Grow up to become like your father; the princes hate him, but the gods do not, for he loves his country" (Scene 10). Even the heroic Thusnelda reaches into the action of the play from without when sending word to Hermann from captivity not to undertake anything for her sake which might harm their country; i.e., to put patriotism above his personal love.

Chorus and dance contribute further to alleviate the ominous mood which broods so heavily over the second play of this trilogy.

"*Hermanns Tod,*" a 'bardiet' in 23 scenes, has been called an "Alterswerk"—a product of the poet's old age. However, that should not be said in any derogative sense at all. For this last play actually is by far the best one of the cycle. The hero's character appears much more individualized and finely drawn. The Hermann-Thusnelda relationship is one of moving beauty, while the picture of the final isolation of the hero reaches truly tragic heights. Moreover, all these people live, breathe and act like human beings and not like so many embodiments of principles. Even an occasional touch of humor alleviates the grim atmosphere of the plot.

The 'bardiet' depicts the civil war, with its final revolt against Hermann himself, some years after the defeat described in the preceding play. The hero is now besieged in his own home. He has been wounded in battle, and a faithful young companion, Horst (Hermann's Horatio), tends to his injuries as the play opens. Through the frank exchange between these two we are introduced to the present situation. We learn of the hopelessness of Hermann's stand. We hear that Marbod had conquered half of Germany; but also that Hermann has fought him successfully, that Marbod has had to flee to Italy; that Ingomar had joined Marbod out of hate for the hero. Now Ingomar has started a revolt against Hermann even among his Cheruscans by spreading the suspicion of Hermann's aspirations for hegemony over all of Germany. (Here Klopstock follows closely Tacitus' report of Arminius' end).

That Segestes has promptly joined the revolt and even may

be plotting murder, does not surprise the hero. But that his favorite, young Katwald, could become convinced of Hermann's despotic intentions and, therefore, has joined the enemy camp, grieves Hermann most; whereupon Horst, "Katwald is noble and only misled, he is not evil" (Scene 2). Now Horst urges Hermann to flee, as he is completely outnumbered. But that might appear as admission of guilt. "Never. Rather death than flight," Hermann retorts. (Scenes 3 & 7.) In Scene 6, however, the exhausted, sleeping hero reveals what he dared not tell when awake: he still dreams of entering Rome as victor! To this end, and to this end alone, has he tried to force all Germans into a temporary union. But once Rome is humbled, "all tribes shall be free"—once more Klopstock touches upon Tacitus' implied conception of Arminius' end.

At this critical juncture Thusnelda is expected home from captivity and Theude, their son, has set out to meet his mother. While siege and battle proceed—while messengers come and go and Hermann nurses his bleeding wounds, he also prepares for Thusnelda's reception and has the care of the wounded at heart: despite imminent danger to his person, the welfare of his family, of his warriors and people are his only concern. Thusnelda's return and Hermann's endeavor to conceal from her, for one brief moment of happiness, the truth of their desperate situation—that she has returned to perish with him—is one of the highest points in Klopstock's entire trilogy (Scene 13). The trial of the hero as 'instigator of the ruin of Varus' innocent Romans,' and 'as the cause of Germany's sufferings at the hands of an insulted Rome,' is a pathetic travesty of truth, indeed. In the course of the mock-trial, the ugly conspiracy almost breaks up when the traitors face the innocent hero (Scene 13). Now Katwald returns openly to Hermann's side in order to atone for his error by dying for and with his idol. Soon Gambriv follows his example (Scene 20). Gambriv even attempts to save Thusnelda from her impending fate. There is, furthermore, the touching offer of the simple country folk, who have come to welcome Thusnelda, to take up arms in their hero's behalf. Those are touching moments in view of the utter hopelessness of Hermann's situation. They underline the tragedy which culminates in the utter destruction of Hermann's house and faction; a tragedy so sweeping, so vengeful and complete, that it fills even the Roman witnesses with awe and horror.

But Klopstock's gods are just: in the avalanche which the wicked have unleashed, the guilty are swept away with the innocent.

VI. THE STRUGGLE FOR NATIONAL FREEDOM AND UNION.

Heinrich von Kleist and His Successors.

While Klopstock's patriotism stems primarily from the poet's inmost experience of mother-tongue and native cultural tradition, Kleist's patriotic passion has its main roots in the political chaos of his turbulent age. It is steeped in wrathful indignation. His "Hermannsschlacht", which a leading Kleist scholar of our time[1] rightly calls 'lurid and greatly overrated' is, nevertheless, a powerful document of the spirit of its era—a perfect example of the two-edged nature of nationalism: passionate love of one's country and an equally fervent hate of the foreign. Moreover, as this play was written hastily as forceful propaganda for a specific situation—"it is meant for the present", the poet states— its conciseness and dramatic merits bear witness to its author's skill.

Yet in complete contrast to the enthusiastic though 'naive' poet Klopstock, with whom Kleist shared the 'grosse Vaterlandsgedanke,' Heinrich von *Kleist* (1777-1811) was of a highly complex nature, a man of ever-present and perilous psychic tensions. Soldier, philosopher, poet and patriot, he harbored elements of both Hamlet and Fortinbras within his sensitive soul. The Prussian ethos of duty and the love of letters were his family heritage. But he also was a restless rover of the Celtis and Hutten type. As a keen, idealistic realist with considerable romantic proclivities, his own life bore all the elements of dramatic heroism and ended prematurely in tragedy. Lack of recognition as an artist and grief over his country's fate drove one of Germany's greatest dramatic talents to an untimely grave.

Yet Kleist was not a born patriotic zealot nor a political agitator from the start. Far from it. The young thinker begins as a disciple of Kant, as a devotee of the world of the abstract. Like the humanists he dreams of a poet's calm and seclusion until, under the hammer-blows of the Corsican's advances, his patriotic conscience is aroused and draws him irresistibly into the maelstrom of political events. In a letter to his sister in 1806 we get a first inkling of what is in store for the unpolitical soldier-poet when he indignantly exclaims, *"We* are the subjugated peoples of the Romans." The first victory of the Austrians over Napoleon at Aspern, in 1809, raises Kleist's hopes high for one brief moment—only to let him sink again to the very depths of despair under the ensuing catastrophic events.

In this spirit he plans to found a patriotic journal with the challenging title of 'Germania' (1809). It was meant as a rallying-point for genuine patriots, as a flaming 'J'accuse' and protest against national disgrace and injury. It never reached the printer's press. But some of his intended contributions have been preserved. They, above all else, reflect the spirit which also animates the poet's "Hermannsschlacht" (1808).

In his short story "Michael Kohlhaas" (1804/05), Kleist had shown the individual's fight for justice from a partial state. In his drama "The Prince of Homburg" (1810), he was to depict the individual's education in a new, ethical citizenship. But in his patriotic essays, as in his "Hermannsschlacht", the soul of a nation is aroused to a struggle for survival and to a fight for 'Mankind's greatest good'—Liberty.

The introduction to the 'Germania' opens as follows: "This journal is meant to be a first breath of life of German freedom— It shall proclaim what, under French pressure of the last three agonizing years, could not be uttered: all our anxiety, our hopes, our misery and happiness—"

Also meant for publication in the 'Germania' journal was his "Catechism of the Germans—After the Spanish Model[2], for Children and Adults." This is a dialogue in 16 terse chapters and, with its sharp-edged succinctness, quite worthy of a fighting Hutten. The 13 chapters which have been preserved bear the following revealing titles: 1) On Germany in General; 2) On the Love of One's Country; 3) The Ruin of Germany; 4) The Arch-enemy; 5) On Germany's Rebirth; 6) The German War upon France; 7) On Admiring Napoleon; 8) On Educating the Germans; 9) A Side-issue; 10) On the German Constitution; 13) On Voluntary Contributions; 14) On Highest Officials; 15) On Treason; 16) Finale.

This 'Catechism' is a highly effective exchange of queries and answers between a father and his son. It opens with the parent's pertinent question: Tell me, my child, who are you. The boy replies: I am a German. Though I was born a Saxon, my fatherland, to which Saxony belongs, is Germany—. To the father's retort that the boy must be dreaming, for has not Napoleon broken up Germany? the boy asserts that Germany still lives in the common will of her people to resist the Corsican conqueror. And *why* has the conqueror so wantonly destroyed Germany? Because he is a spirit of evil, a detestable being; one who marks the beginning of the bad and the end of the good; a sinner whom to accuse neither the breath of men nor that of the angels would ever suffice. But why do the Germans endure such insult and sufferings so long? Because—and this sounds like a note of self-confession—they love too much to reflect when, instead, they should feel and act. Thus they have lost sight of Man's highest goods. And what are Mankind's highest goods? God, Fatherland, the Emperor, Freedom, Love and Loyalty, Beauty, Knowledge and the Arts. In short what the poet pleads for is the right synthesis of objectivity and subjectivity—of a patriotism proven by sterling deeds, *plus* culture and humaneness. For—Kleist continues his argument—he who can neither love nor hate belongs into the nethermost regions of hell: the lukewarm patriots of words who want in deeds. What, then, is the German's most pressing task now? To take up arms at once and to emulate the example of Spaniards and Tyrolese in their glorious fight for freedom—to destroy Frenchmen wherever they are encountered ravaging abroad. But what must he do whom God has blessed with earthly goods? He must gladly sacrifice everything he can do without. And what is that? All but water and bread and the garment that clothes his nakedness. For gold and earthly goods are as nothing now when compared with what shall be gained by their sacrifices, namely—national freedom. What does he do who refuses to follow the emperor's call to arms? He commits national treason. But treason is an abomination in the eyes of the Lord, for the Lord loves him who dies for his liberty; He detests the knavish soul.

Once more the essence of this flaming document is touched upon in another essay likewise intended for the 'Germania' journal. It bears the title: "What Is at Stake in This War?" The answer in brief: the sacred community of a glorious, free and innocent nation which is threatened by a foreign invader's wicked aspirations for violent world domination. A national communion is in jeopardy which, by its own merits, belongs to all mankind and whose extinction no German breast could ever survive; though it could only be wiped out in streams of blood before which the sun itself would pale.

The spirit of these stormy essays pulsates in Kleist's "Hermannsschlacht," too. Although Germany's patriotic literature of the Napoleonic era is full of stern calls to duty, seldom has the demand for total sacrifice in times of national crisis been sounded with such uncompromising finality as by Kleist.

To be sure, Schiller, too, had called from the stage for a heroic attitude on the part of the entire nation. As early as 1801, in his "Jungfrau von Orleans", Dunois pleads with his faint-hearted king:

Nichtswürdig ist die Nation, die nicht
Ihr alles freudig setzt an ihre Ehre[3].

And, once more, in his "Wilhelm Tell" (1804) which also is a most forceful outcry 'In Tyrannos' and a fervent plea for national unity:

Nein, eine Grenze hat Tyrannenmacht![4]

Indeed, Schiller's entire Tell play revolves about the famous Rütli oath of the Swiss leaders who are about to revolt:

Wir wollen sein ein einzig Volk von Brüdern,
In keiner Not uns trennen und Gefahr[5],

while their venerable leader, ancient Attinghausen, with the vision of final victory in his dying heart, leaves his co-patriots with this urgent bequest:

Seid einig, einig, einig![6]

Though doubtless inferior in dramatic merits when compared with Schiller's patriotic masterpiece, Kleist's Hermann drama is even of a sterner mettle and, hence, hardly inferior in directness and force of propaganda, though it is centered largely upon Tell's proud trust in individual self-reliance:

Der Starke ist am mächtigsten *allein*.[7]

It even seems as if Kleist's Hermann had learned from the tragic handicaps of Klopstock's lonely hero, as he hardly ever is hampered by the half-heartedness and quarrelsome selfishness of his German brothers in arms. It is his own superior farsightedness, his indomitable personal will, his shrewd calculations and heroic personal risks that lead to German victory. In this, Kleist follows Tacitus' descriptions most closely.

One even could say that, in this song-of-songs of hate, moral principles are intentionally thrown to the wind, or at least largely sacrificed. But in the lack of moral scruples towards the national foe, this Hermann play again reflects the spirit of its age, when ethical considerations towards the invader appear consumed in a glowing hatred and in the desperate urge for survival. Kleist's famous war song entitled "Germania an Ihre Kinder," also of the year 1809, culminates in this characteristic outcry:

>Schlagt ihn tot! Das Weltgericht
>Fragt nach euren Gründen nicht![8]

For the wanton breaker of the peace among nations and of all moral laws deserves not otherwise!

Thus it is not surprising that Kleist has also removed most of the vestiges of gentility and magnanimity which previous generations had bestowed upon the early hero and his life companion. Instead, Kleist has given to his heroic fighter a wellnigh demonic character. Although this Cheruscan ruler receives the Roman legate while seated on his throne and even displays an occasional liking for Oriental ease and splendor—while his Thusnelda plays the lute and flirts with the young Roman noble in the Roman fashion—these, too, are calculated features in the German hero's preconceived designs. The spirit of the whole is intentionally primitive again, as are the instincts of these early Germans who must serve as a mask for Kleist's demands on his own hard-pressed generation. Attinghausen's bold resolve in Schiller's "Tell" is no less Hermann's:

>Sie sollen kommen, uns ein Joch aufzwingen,
>Das wir entschlossen sind *nicht* zu ertragen![9]

This singleness of purpose is furthermore quite strikingly brought out by the inner structure of Kleist's political play and by the choice of its motifs. Here every traditional feature that does not serve its one propagandistic purpose is eliminated from the plot. Gone are the motifs of the rivalries between and within the leading families. Only the protracted antagonism between Hermann and Marbod has survived—though it precedes the dramatic action and appears considerably mellowed. For it even ends in close cooperation and final harmony. This time we hear nothing of Hermann's parents, of the arrant Segestes and his vacillating son, Siegismund. Even Flavius, and with him the effective motif of the hostile brothers, has been discarded. So is Thusnelda's intense agony over her contested marriage and over the rivalries among her various, unequal suitors. All this has

been subdued to the mild flirtation with the young **Roman** legate, Ventidius—though Thusnelda's heart does not remain entirely unaffected. But this amorous interlude, too, is shrewdly promoted by the coldly calculating hero himself and thus becomes part of the final Roman catastrophy. Actually almost everything of importance in the plot of this play has its roots in the cautious plans of this sagacious Cheruscan. He is the master of farsighted calculated risks and, hence, of unfailingly effective deceptions. In short, he is the model hero of Kleist's patriotic "Catechism", willing to stake his all for German freedom—his crown, his person and possessions, even his children and the tranquillity of his Thusnelda's heart. This unique inner independence and even aloofness from his immediate surroundings sets Kleist's Hermann off from all previous Arminius versions:
Allein muss ich in solchem Kampfe stehn.[10]
Political expedience and compromise are not his nature: he strives for everything or nothing—total victory or death. He is, indeed, of a demonic nature; a man to whom deceitful Rome—though Hermann certainly has learned from her—has no equal.

Kleist's play in 5 Acts is built up on two triangle themes. There is, first, the Rome-Hermann-Marbod struggle; and secondly the Hermann-Thusnelda-Ventidius plot. They form, as it were, a major and a minor theme and finally blend.

The Romans have tried to play the mighty Suevian leader, Marbod, against his Cheruscan antagonist—though not yet with decisive success. Now they plan to increase their pressure by inciting Hermann against Marbod. They intend to promise the Cheruscan their full support and, eventually, the German crown under the protectorate of Rome. But Hermann anticipates their plan; he sees through their deceitful divide-and-conquer scheme. He knows that Germany's only chance of survival lies in a solid union of her divergent and competitive parts. To bring such unity about, Hermann must, above all, convince Marbod of his own absolute sincerity and win the suspicious competitor over as an ally: truthfulness, mutual respect and unselfish cooperation are as indispensable to national victory and freedom, as the art of dissembling and misleading is imperative in the struggle with the treacherous common foe.

At this point Kleist's play opens. An uneasy peace prevails. Some German princes are hunting-guests at Hermann's court.

Imperiled or already injured in their respective territories, the princes attempt to lure Hermann into an alliance against Rome. The Cheruscan seems indifferent to their plight; he refuses. He knows that the selfish and quarrelsome spirit of these princes is Rome's most powerful ally. Hence he is forced to bury his own plans within his heart. He does not dare to share his secrets until the time is ripe for a swift, concerted, decisive blow. Meanwhile, let them assume he is about to lead them against Marbod.

Soon the scene changes to the second theme: the Hermann-Thusnelda-Ventidius plot. This Ventidius appears as an envoy from his emperor: Hermann is to admit the Roman legions as allies into his country. They, in turn, shall join him in his present contest with Marbod. If the Cheruscans are successful, German hegemony will fall to them as their just reward.

Hermann seems quite honored and eager to accept. His German guests are appalled at the prospect of Hermann's gradual submission to Roman occupation as they weigh its consequences for themselves.

Meantime the triumphant Ventidius whiles the time away courting the fair wife of this indulgent Cheruscan. But Hermann secretly plans his strategy. A swift messenger is quietly dispatched to Marbod's court. He shall reveal Rome's treacherous designs, together with Hermann's urgent proposals for speedy, concerted counteraction. Hermann's own two sons—plus a dagger against these innocent hostages, should the Suevian detect but a trace of deceit in their father's plea—must convince and win over the old political rival. Even more: Hermann assures Marbod of his personal homage and future submission to Suevian leadership once freedom is won. This hero trusts in the justice of his course and, hence, on the help of the gods. He knows neither doubt nor inner conflict.

Although Attarin, Marbod's chief counsellor, warns against the cunning Cheruscan as a "deceived deceiver" and favors cooperation with Rome, the innocent trust of Hermann's sons, plus the Romans' sudden and secret departure from Marbod's court, carry the day: Marbod sets out at once to cross the Weser river. Hermann will follow behind the Roman legions to the Teutoburg Forest. At a given date and signal the Romans shall be attacked on all sides and be destroyed in the inclement swamps and woods.

While these preparations are in progress, Varus enters Cheruscia. His ravaging cohorts proceed with axe and torch and sword. Still Hermann feigns eagerness for the proffered alliance with Rome. Varus is received with regal pomp though also in a spirit of proper submissiveness. The Cheruscan even pleads for the lives of those ravagers whom Varus orders killed. Actually, these Roman excesses delight his heart, for they play straightway into his hands. Even the rape of an innocent girl by the marauding soldiers is welcome news for his plans. Trusted Cheruscans in Roman disguise are sent over all the land in order to inflame the populace further: a mortal hate for the national foe must now be fanned even in the faintest German heart!

But any suspicion against Hermann on Varus' part is quickly dispelled by the trusting courter of Thusnelda. Has not Ventidius won the first victory over the barbarian when he carried off Thusnelda's lock as a gift for his empress and, with it, Thusnelda's heart?

Yet Cheruscan revenge is as pitiless as it is swift and demonic. Before Hermann sets out in the rear of the Roman army, he sees to it that the massacre of the entire foreign garrison left behind in his land will be properly carried out. Moreover, he does not leave for Varus' destruction without gaining a victory over the heart of Thusnelda who is pleading to save young Ventidius. But his letter with her lock has been intercepted. As her two-faced suitor's designs are revealed, Thusnelda's shame and anger know no bounds. While Varus and his legions march to their fate, Ventidius is left to Thusnelda's savage revenge: at the midnight hour the hopeful lover is handed over to the embraces of a hungry bear. Thusnelda herself leads Ventidius into the animal's cage. Scorning all pleas of her horrified servants and the cries of the victim of her injured pride, she hurls the key away into the night. Her mission fulfilled, she swoons and sinks to the ground—

Meanwhile the Roman legions are marching in circles through the storm-racked woods. They are at the point of exhaustion. Their German guides pretend to know no longer where they are. The elements of nature seem to have joined in the conspiracy. In the ominous gloaming, an Alraune[11] steps into Varus' path. To his half-mocking questions: Whence do I come? Whither do I go? and Where am I? he hears her mocking replies: "From nothingness; to nothingness; two steps from thy grave, close between nothing and nothing."

With that Varus' spirit seems broken. Messages of desertion pour in from all sides. Marbod confronts Varus, ready to attack; Hermann stands in his rear. Thus a battle ensues which ends in a massacre as merciless as its outcome is inexorable and sweeping. Over the bodies of their fallen foes Hermann and Marbod clasp hands for an oath of lasting loyalty and friendship: East and West, North and South stand united, ready to face the future of a re-liberated Germany.

There can be little doubt that Kleist's Marbod stands for Austria and his Hermann for Prussia. But it is also significant that Kleist makes Marbod win the decisive Varus battle, while Hermann arrives almost too late. Moreover, Marbod generously rejects Hermann's homage and, in turn, proposes the young Cheruscan as the future German leader. However, the settlement of this important question seems intentionally left open: it is to be decided by a popular vote among all Germans.

As the Austrian officer, von Ayrenhoff, once had looked to the Prussian king, Frederick II, for hegemony in a united Germany, so the Prussian officer, von Kleist, in view of the weakness and indecision on the part of the Prussian state, looks again to the Austrian emperor for leadership: In Trinitate Robur!

It is obvious that Kleist's "Hermannsschlacht" is a political drama rather than a social play. Hence its paucity of warm emotions and genuinely human relationships. Even the Hermann-Thusnelda relation, which had inspired some earlier Arminius poets to interpretations of real warmth and beauty, suffers from Kleist's one-sided approach. Here the hero stands quite isolated, and to such a degree that not even Thusnelda dares to participate in his secret plans and hopes. She, too, is moved about, as by a superior player, in a half calculated and half playful manner: a figure among others on the strategist's political chess board. Her main features are a fervent love and devotion and its psychic opposite, an equally fervent hate which, once her female pride is injured, does not shrink from utmost cruelty.

Conversely, it is equally characteristic of Kleist's nature that his Varus figure does not lack traces of nobility, despite the poet's glowing hate for the French invader who stands behind this Roman general. But the truly 'Grossmütige' is here the Suevian leader, Marbod, who finally puts aside his long-cherished ambitions and points to Hermann—the real victor over Varus, for his single will has saved the nation from destruction—as the one most worthy of the crown of the united nation.

With Hermann's solemn promise of unrelenting and concerted efforts for the safety of this nation, Kleist brings his play to a triumphant conclusion.

It is part of the distressing tragedy of Kleist's personal life that his patriotic play was almost ignored by his own generation. One did not even risk the printing, much less the performance of it. The drama was not given until 1861, fifty years after its author's death. Its manuscripts circulated clandestinely, and the saddened poet wrote on one of them:
> Wehe, mein Vaterland, dir! Die Leier zum Ruhm dir zu schlagen,
> Ist, getreu dir im Schoss, mir, deinem Dichter, verwehrt.[12]

To Kleist this 'Vaterland,' which means the total German nation, is no longer an exalted dream. It is an 'ideal postulate' and, to his heart, a cherished living reality. What Walter Silz states of Kleist's Hermann figure holds equally true of the poet himself. He, too, is "a genius, a man of vision who pursues an ideal undaunted and undeflected by an unappreciative or hostile world"[13]. This, however, should be applied with one reservation, for, while Hermann "perverts his naturally mild and just character"[14] in the process of achieving his end, his author does not do so to his own. With his transition from the aesthetic cosmopolitanism which dominates his youth to the national patriotism of his manhood, Kleist rediscovers and defines the ethical relationship of the individual to his state *and* his nation. Thus this Hermann grows into a symbolic unifier and savior of his entire people and, therewith, Kleist's drama rises to the stature of a prophetic mythos of the political unity of all Germany.

During the course of the nineteenth century after Kleist's death, the Arminius theme gains steadily in use and popularity. But as the stream widens, it loses in depth. The year 1807 had seen the appearance of a 'Thusnelda' journal dedicated to studies in Germanics which the romanticists fostered assiduously. A second journal with similar archaeological and patriotic purport appeared in 1814 under the name of 'Hermann.' In 1816, a first attempt at a modern Arminius biography was published. Its author, L. Steckling, undertook to present a popular though reliable account of the hero's life according to Roman sources. He traced early Germanic history from the first appearance of the Cimbri and Teutons up to the death of the Cheruscan victor over Varus.

From then on Arminius epics, dramas, and novels pour forth in steady abundance. This flow reaches its climax at the time of the founding of the German empire, in 1871, and of the erection of the Arminius Monument in the Teutoburg Forest, which was dedicated in 1875.

Yet, after Grabbe, the Arminius literature has achieved only little that moves on a significant literary level. Its products mainly reflect on the past and bask in the glory of the newly-won national union and greatness. Political pride rather than patriotic and moral concern—which once had engendered such wide and often noble perspectives—swell the writers' sails, while the lack of great purpose increasingly narrows their views.

Thus the theme gradually ceases to carry a true message and *Arminius has fulfilled the cycle of his national mission.*

However, a few more real poets of the earlier nineteenth century deserve attention: first *Fouqué* and *Grabbe*.

Between Kleist's political plays and Grabbe's daring dramatic sketch stands the work of a once widely-read member of the circle of Berlin romanticists whose Arminius version, though comprehensive and bold, has long since been forgotten.

Friedrich, Baron de LaMotte *Fouqué* (1777-1843) was, like Kleist, a son of the Prussian aristocracy, a man of similar aims and ideals and one of Kleist's personal friends. The scion of an old Norman-French noble family, he was a god-child of the great King Frederick himself by virtue of the military merits of his sires. Like Kleist he was a soldier, a born poet, a great patriot, and a romanticist. As a volunteer he took part in the War of Liberation and beheld the downfall of the Corsican adventurer, which Kleist had not been destined to witness.

Fouqué's poetic imagination ranged freely from romantic adventure stories, from lyrical, patriotic and spiritual poems to epics, fairy tales and patriotic plays. Though remembered today only for his unique "Undine" tale—one of the finest flowers of German poetic romanticism—Fouqué dreamt for years of a dramatization of the entire German national and the Prussian history in a series of plays. He thus anticipated similar aims of Grabbe's and those of Gustav Freytag's "Bilder aus der deutschen Vergangenheit" (1862) and "Die Ahnen" (1880).

However, the theater was not Fouqué's element and his *"Hermann, ein Heldenspiel in 4 Abenteuern"*, of the year 1818,— though drawn on a grandiose canvas—shared the fate of most of Fouqué's dramas: it never reached the stage, while Kleist's plays gained steadily in weight and popularity.

Fouqué's ambitious though insignificant *"Atlsächsischer Bildersaal"* (Old Saxon Picture Gallery), which contains the poet's Hermann 'Heldenspiel', made its appearance in 1818. Riffert remarks that the play reflects Fouqué's elation over the national victory at Leipzig. Indeed, while Kleist extols the hate of foreign despotism and proclaims the justness of the struggle for freedom at all costs, Fouqué glorifies the war's successful conclusion. The spirit of reaction and of wide-spread political disillusion and unrest, which followed so swiftly on the heels of the momentous victory, is still absent from it.

However, Riffert also points out that the "Bildersaal", which was planned as early as 1812, was originally not intended as a poetic work at all. It was meant to prepare German youth for the great patriotic task which lay ahead by a better understanding and appreciation of their ancient history and heroes. As the author puts it in his introduction: "Originating in the days of national humiliation and crisis", it shall be "a challenge and offer solace". The swiftness of political events overtook the play's delayed completion.

Riffert is equally right when he calls Fouqué's dramatic poem quite an unusual piece of work. It stands in the shadow of Shakespeare, Klopstock and Kleist; a "moving panegyric" in praise of the great Leipzig Battle, despite its many bizarre elements and grotesque distortions.

Fouqué divides his heroic play into a *Prelude* and *4 Adventures*. He does not depict the Varus battle, as Kleist had done, but opens with a celebration of Hermann's victory at the sixth anniversary of Varus' downfall. Fouqué introduces again many of those elements which Kleist had purposely eliminated from his plot. The inner division of Germany, the short-sightedness and selfishness of her leaders form Fouqué's major motifs. The evil machinations of Segestes cast their shadow already over the victory celebration of the Prelude as he plots with Marbod's envoy against Hermann.

In *Adventure I* Germanicus stands on the Rhine while Segestes abducts Thusnelda. Hermann, in turn, lays siege to his father-in-law's castle. The Roman general soon releases him but both Segestes and Thusnelda are sent to Italy. Hermann subsequently defeats Germanicus on the Werra river and compels him to retreat to the Rhine.

In *Adventure II* Hermann proposes an alliance with Marbod against Rome. However, the suspicious political rival refuses. Before a second encounter with the Romans on the Weser river the hostile brothers, Hermann and Flavius, meet once more. Through the arbitrary interference of Ingomar, Hermann's uncle, the battle (Tacitus' battle of Idistavisus) is lost. Hermann is wounded and flees while Germanicus retreats into Gaul.

Adventure III takes up the final struggle between Hermann and the despotic Marbod, whom some of his followers soon forsake in favor of the juster Cheruscan leader. Conversely, jealousy of his powerful nephew drives Ingomar over to the side of the enemy. This serious setback almost wrecks Hermann's strategic success though, in the end, Marbod is vanquished and forced to relinquish Germany.

The Adventure culminates in an idyllic scene laid in Ravenna where Thusnelda languishes in captivity in the company of her young son, Thumelicus, and Hermann's nephew, Italus.

Adventure IV portrays the tragic end of the Cheruscan warrior. Hermann is now the most powerful ruler in Germany. In order to attack Rome directly and to free his captured family, Hermann strives to unite all Germany under his personal military leadership. But here the arrant Segestes enters once more. He has fled from Italy and at a war council with the reconciled Ingomar and Hermann, Segestes suddenly slays the unsuspecting hero of German freedom.

So far Fouqué has not introduced any essentially new elements into the traditional plot. However—perhaps in order to alleviate the somber effect of his play or to give it a broader and more promising perspective—the romanticist Fouqué suddenly takes a unique and truly amazing turn by linking the pagan-heroic theme with the triumphant rise of Christianity. Thusnelda and the children have become converted in Italy. The voice of the dying Thusnelda reaches the hero before his own death and bids him exchange the glory of Valhalla for the blessedness of the heavenly Redeemer: Christianity and Germandom, the two future conquerors of the world of Rome, blend in a vision and point towards a new age when hostile principles and peoples will stand reconciled.

Christian Dietrich *Grabbe* (1801-'36) represents another truly tragic case in the history of German drama: a born talent prematurely wasted; a man of robust native strength, proud and ambitious, but also of bizarre caprices. His psychic pendulum perpetually oscillated between emotional extremes, and want of moral discipline doomed him early.

When Tieck read Grabbe's first play he immediately recognized its unique passionateness and the boldness of its diction, but he promptly added: "the gruesome is not tragic; wild, coarse cynicism is not irony and convulsions do not betray strength."

Grabbe's *"Hermannsschlacht"*, the last of his dramatic works—unfinished despite repeated revisions and published posthumously in 1838—still reflects the same basic weaknesses together with the untimely decline of a technical genius.

Here Grabbe's obstinate eccentricity goes utterly astray when he attempts to perform an impossible feat. For he actually suggests presenting the protracted marches and clashes of entire armies within the confining limits of the theater stage. On the other hand, this "Hermannsschlacht" offers considerably more than a picture of the Varus battle. Here are the rudiments of any number of feasible plays—but not one uniform drama.

Moreover, the sacred exaltation of Klopstock's patriotism and the justifiable patriotic wrath of Kleist's generation did not guide Grabbe's pen. Neither the forceful expulsion of a wanton invader, nor Fouqué's elation over a great victory won, nor the urgent call for stern punishment of the national oppressor out of an injured sense of justice, such as Klopstock, Kleist and Fouqué had voiced, give force and form to Grabbe's scenes. To be sure, Grabbe stresses this third motif as the main incentive of the ancient Teutonic revolt. Actually, however, the anger over the French oppressor had already given way in wide circles of Grabbe's generation to a romantic adulation of the dazzling Caesar of yesterday who was fast growing into a heroic legend. Thus Grabbe's version of the 'Hermannsschlacht' theme is predominantly a satirical one. He even lends to the traditional plot a biting bourgeois note. For Grabbe largely divests his intended 'Nationalspiel' of its former national color. He provincializes it with a marked regional hue. Moreover, with this dramatic sketch the failing poet Grabbe bids a nostalgic farewell to his Westphalian homeland. In the process, he becomes a co-founder of Westphalia's 'Heimatkunst'—a literary genre which soon flourished in other parts of Germany as well. Local topography and regional cultural traits of his own day engage this 'Hermann' author just as much as do the strategic aspects and the far-reaching results of the historic Varus battle of the year 9 A.D.

Grabbe's satire, on the other hand, aims primarily at the renewed calamitous oppression of the German people—though this time not by a wanton intruder from without but at the hands of their own, hereditary and reactionary leaders. The invigorating storm of the popular uprisings of 1812/13—this grandiose spectacle of the wrath of a protesting nation, of a "Volk in Waffen"—had long since subsided pitiably. Great political perspectives had shrunken again to Philistine proportions as princes trembled while their subjects grumbled. Therefore Grabbe's 'Hermann' play reverts again to the primordial roots of strength of this uneasy nation—to the perennial vigor and rigor of its peasant world: Grabbe's Hermann is "to show greatness in a paltry age"[15]. But does he? The poet has obviously failed in his hopes, for his 17 scenes, epic and at times even lyrical in nature, are too often wanting in cogency and dynamic force. The constant flow of 'asides' impedes the dramatic effect still further and creates the impression of a revoltingly double-tongued treacherousness on the part of the supposedly heroic national liberator.

The very structure of this 'drama' betrays its basically epic character, for Grabbe divides it into an Introduction (Prologue), 3 Days and 3 Nights of Battle (with subdivisions), and an Epilogue which plays abroad—in Rome. But, worst of all: Grabbe simply superimposes some features of his contemporary peasant world upon the tribal sphere of Arminius' day. He even employs modern family names for his primitive warriors. The princely Hermann himself is turned into a 'Bauernführer' of the Attinghausen type in Schiller's "Wilhelm Tell"—though Hermann certainly is wanting in the tempered wisdom and integrity of Schiller's venerable sage. Princess Thusnelda, on the other hand, dutifully performs the trying functions of the absent country squire's spouse in kitchen, home and barn; though she also bears some features of a Northern Amazon and is quite able to put her country's welfare far above all human relationships. As to other German figures, Grabbe carries his profaning realism so far as to paint his average Germans largely as rogues, as poachers, as lazy and deceitful among themselves, as excessively given to drinking, gambling and every conceivable debauchery. No wonder Grabbe's Roman praetors and scribes harbor scant respect for such enemies. Instead of burning with the fire of liberty, their leaders either find it hard to restrain them or even have to humor these fellows and coax them into disciplined action.

And what about these tribal leaders who surround Grabbe's Arminius?

When the great battle is finally won and Hermann suggests continued concerted military action against Rome until permanent peace and freedom are assured as the fruits of such costly victories—when he points to common security which is to be gained only from national unity under one leader and crown, then he is promptly rebuffed and suspected by these head-strong and tribal-minded particularists. For they are war-weary and much too eager to disband and go home. Hence the liberator's vision of their common national destiny must be buried in a post-battle feast and drinking-bout.

Thus a potentially great play comes to an end—not only in stark satire but even in burlesque banality.

The inner incongruity of this type of struggle for freedom is increased by the Epilogue. Here the emperor in Rome receives the message of Varus' destruction. Augustus is on his deathbed and the simultaneous news of Varus' débâcle *and* of the birth of the Christ child in distant Judaea gives the poisoned clairvoyant his *coup de grâce*. But, viewing this play in its entirety, one is tempted to ask: does the poet thus create a convincing symbol of the vanity of human ambition and endeavors—does he really move ephemeral events into the focus and dimensions of the eternal?

Grabbe's Hermann alone seems to realize how little cause there actually is for the 'terror Teutonicus' which is soon to grip Italy. For he terminates his rôle with this revealing 'aside':

"Aye, if Rome but knew that these people, otherwise so brave, can not see farther ahead than a few miles; that they would rather eat and drink right here at home than set out to destroy her (Rome), she would scarcely tremble at the tidings of my victory as her master, his teeth chattering, is bound to do—"

There is but little to add as to human relationships and characters in this Grabbe play. There are only three figures that deserve being approached as such: Hermann, Thusnelda and Varus. But Grabbe's Hermann talks, reflects and dissembles too much. He resigns himself far too easily. He therefore is not tragic in the end even in view of the apparent failure of his life's mission. Grabbe, no doubt, had lost his old formative power. He was no longer able to translate character traits freely into action as Kleist had done. The downfall of Grabbe's Varus, on the other hand, is not without a tinge of tragedy. He still has the elements of a worthy counterplayer to any poet's Arminius. Proud, courageous, conscious of his duty and honor— a man of iron will and harsh in discipline, he goes down as a victim of Rome's insatiable greed and lust of conquest which underestimates its inner limitations and the potential vigor of its enemies.

Above all, Grabbe clearly demonstrates that Arminius is indeed no symbol for a 'paltry age.' Here he can only hide his true entity in a satirical cloak. Though the dream of national unity did survive, Grabbe's generation as a whole had lost its old idealism. Political vision gone, it also lost its will to sacrifice.

Deprived of these qualities, Arminius' life stands bereft of its true meaning and purpose, and Grabbe's princes can not but refuse their leader's vision, whereas Kleist's Marbod and Hermann freely exchanged their oaths of loyalty in the interest of the common good.

* * * * *

Two truly distinguished names still stand out among the scores of post-Kleistian Arminius authors. Though their attempts remained fragments, their very stature in the field of German art suggests their mention. They are Otto Ludwig and Gerhart Hauptmann.

Otto *Ludwig's* (1813-1865) intense interest in the Arminius story dates back to the years 1849-1851. It must have had its origin in the poet's sad disillusion over the failure of the liberal Revolution of 1848.

If we include the early plays of Ludwig's youth, the poet has left us eight finished dramas plus sketches and fragments of thirteen more. The latter were edited in part, and for the first time, by Moritz Heydrich, in 1874. The unfinished Arminius material was never sifted and appraised in its entirety until 1930. Heinrich Kraeger's thorough study of that year throws a new light on Ludwig's painstaking working method. Moreover, it illuminates the irreparable loss of a first-rate German drama; the elements of a play which might have ranked with Goethe's *Goetz* and Schiller's *Wallenstein*.

Kraeger terms it a 'grosser Trümmerhaufen'—a hundred precious chips which, alas, do not result in one big diamond. These 'chips', by some strange stroke of irony, have long lain hidden in the Goethe und Schiller Archiv, at Weimar. For Ludwig, a lifelong student and protagonist of Shakespeare's dramatic genius, was in many of his aesthetic views diametrically opposed to the two giants of German classicism. Not that Ludwig aspired to rival them. He was a man of modesty who liked to call himself the 'precursor of a greater man to come'; he freely recognized the limitations of his talent. But he also was an honest and courageous fighter for his principles.

In his correspondence Ludwig takes issue again and again with the classics of Weimar: "Schiller and Goethe have raised the arbitrariness of their subjectivity to the level of lawgiving"[16]; and once more, to Ambrunn: "It is my aim to introduce again the principle of *manliness*, not only into our German literature, but also into our life—a principle which Schiller and Goethe have entirely removed from it. Their poetry embraces only one side of human nature—the female side; i.e., the virtues of their heroes are negative and womanish: self-restraint, decorum, and dignity. But there is no room with them for those passions ('Affekte') which Kant has termed the brave ('wackere') and truly manly ones—neither in their practice nor in their theory. Schiller's philosophy knows only one kind of human greatness—the passive one"[17].

As Kleist before him, so Ludwig envisions the salvation of his age in a new dedication to vigorous, unselfish action, not in reflection. He is equally, or even more, at odds with the political poets of his agitated age who 'degrade poetry by making it the hand-maiden of political and social propaganda'[18].

It certainly may be claimed that this Ludwig does not lag behind the spirit of his time—he stands above it. He sets his ideals high indeed; and, for his own artistic work, almost beyond reach. Thus this born poet, who equals the greatest in range and force of poetic imagination, becomes an inveterate experimenter, often even a procrastinator. His uneventful outer life, harassed by chronic ailing, stands in wellnigh tragic contrast to the richness of his vision and the agitation of his inner being. A heroic fighter for the highest principles, he went through life quite like his own Arminius figure: lonely, often thwarted and misjudged.

From the fragments of Ludwig's Hermann play—there are three different sketches with variants to each—we are able to discern that the poet was driving at a powerful character drama in the Shakespearean vein, which would have moved the play into the mental climate of Grabbe and Kleist. But Ludwig's study of his hero was also to be intensely psychological and tragic.

His Cheruscan is a hero with a splendid vision. Like Tacitus' Arminius, he stands 'head and shoulders above his own people', lonely and misunderstood. In the end he is to perish with his grief of being unable to fulfill his mission: the unification of Germany. In that respect he differs completely from Kleist's and Grabbe's versions. But as he goes down in tragic personal defeat, he knows in his heart that his cause—the cause of truth, justice and freedom—will, of historical necessity, triumph in the end, once his people have come to grasp his vision. Thus he, too, looks upon himself as the forerunner of greater men to come: "Many will have to labour for the great cause"[19]. Thus this Hermann's true enemy is once more the paltry spirit of his age—not the Roman's, not traitorous Inguiomar, Sigmund, or Segestes.

"You are not too big for us—we are too small for you", says Dietmar to the hero who, in the presence of his murderers, points proudly to his heart as 'Freedom's never desecrated temple.' Dying he reconciles his foes and overcomes the envy of old Inguiomar, while the Prophetess concludes the play by pointing at the former enemies, one dead now and the other still alive:

The coward lives—but only to the noble
Is glory given— — .[20]

Ludwig sums up on his psychological purpose in an annotation to his intended final act. Here he says of his Hermann: '—lonely and misunderstood in his greatness; he is carped at and hindered in everything by those for whom he does it; he breaks down and recovers his courage; he forces the good upon those who will not have it and perishes over it; the man whose, fate it is to be ahead of his time'.

As such he shares the tragic lot of Grabbe's Hermann and even of Schiller's Marquis Posa in *Don Carlos*.

Thus the poet labored with devotion, yet without the final triumph of completion, over 'a topic for all; a form for the many; and a substance for the best'[21].

In the case of *Gerhart Hauptmann* (1862-1946) we may be considerably briefer, as little has come, or is known, of his youthful ambitions in the field of Arminius literature. But we do hear that, at the age of twenty, Hauptmann planned a Hermann epic in twenty cantos; besides a drama with the title of "Germanen und Römer", also with Arminius in the central rôle.

Paul Schlenther[22] records a statement by Hauptmann from those early days which expresses the young history student's intention 'to wander forsaken paths to the dim antiquity of our people'. According to von Hülsen[23], this short-lived decision was inspired by the recitations of the popular bard, Wilhelm Jordan.

Schlenther reports further that only one and one half of the twelve epic cantos were finished in manuscript, whereas the Hermann drama apparently never outgrew the planning stage. The versatile mind of the artist-student soon was drawn into other channels. Even the centennial celebrations of the Wars of Liberation could not revive the full-grown playwright's interest in the Arminius story. In 1913, he offered his people his ill-fancied "Festival in German Rhymes" instead.

CONCLUSION: SURVEY OF THE LAST DECADES.

Power-Nation and Expansion.

As previously mentioned, towards the end of the 19th century the Arminius motif descends to the level of a favorite with an era of patriotic festivals commemorating past events of local, regional, or national importance.

The Franco-Prussian War of 1870, culminating as it did in the long-delayed foundation of the German empire, quite naturally engendered a considerable wave of national pride and patriotism. The year of the dedication of the Hermann Monument as a national shrine in the heart of the Teutoburg Forest (1875) also marks the birth of our modest Arminius 'philology'. The year 1909 witnessed the celebrations of the nineteen hundredth anniversary of the fateful Varus Battle. The nation-wide centennial festivals commemorating the Wars of Liberation, in 1913, also lent to the Arminius motif a renewed lease on life. Then, in World War I, Germany's first national hero serves once more in his rôle as a warner, a unifier in spirit, and as the extoller of German virtues and the common will to sacrifice[1]. The national socialists, on the other hand, gave to the Arminius theme its latest, often so ugly and repugnant turn by hailing the distant tribal warrior as the father of German racial consciousness and of overbearing self-assertion.

It could hardly be termed accidental that these sympathizers of the new *Bewegung* turned to the novel as their favorite medium for celebrating Arminius. Its looser form and wider scope lends itself more readily than any play could do to the presentation of the hero's entire ife. Furthermore, the novel offers a more effective medium for all-out propaganda[2].

This final period of the Arminius story in German literature is covered by the Sydow dissertation of 1937 which, while reliable enough in facts, is nevertheless of questionable soundness because of its narrowed perspective.

The youthful author wishes to trace 'the metamorphosis of the *Leitidee* and the possible enlargement of the Arminius motif' during the past 130 years, since Kleist.[3] He does so by examining some of the more significant Arminius versions. However, Sydow's major emphasis is placed merely upon the Arminius productions since about 1890, and especially on those of his own time.

Yet, Sydow's criteria are *Volkswürdigkeit* and *Kunstwertigkeit*. The former seems to signify a kind of racial worthiness in so far as the individual *opus* must reflect and appeal to the highest qualities of the poet's nation. This conviction apparently is shared by most of the Arminius writers of the last two or three decades—a period overcharged with highly self-indulgent, nationalistic emotion. Thus these authors now use the Arminius theme as a medium to further their aggressive pretentions, while the hero himself is celebrated as the founder of the national '*Führer*-principle'[4]—as the first 'German' to possess genuine racial self consciousness and pride, together with the vision of the absolute need for union among all Germans.

On the other hand, the poet must also establish his personal *Volkswürdigkeit* by his sense of responsibility towards his own people. He must display the 'new national-ideological approach' to his nation's history[5].

Sydow, therefore, seems to advocate a *Blut-und-Boden* type of national literature[6] to which Grabbe's Arminius drama, together with his *epigoni* in the field of innocent, patriotic *Heimatdichtung*, could be termed the modest forerunners by historical accident. For these latest writers on Arminius, nationalistically inflamed as they are, extend their dynamic *Heimat*-enthusiasm to their entire race and nation.

It was only natural that Grabbe's theme of the *Volk-Führer-Heimat* relationship should attract and fascinate their frame of mind. Thus they were the first to perform Grabbe's play[7], after a century of its inglorious eclipse.

Their own Cheruscan hero, however, now fights for *Volkwerdung*, and in his heroic struggle this youth beholds, above all, the struggle between the *völkisches*[8] and the dynastic principles. Moreover, for them Arminius finally becomes *a symbol of Germany's destiny per se*—the symbol of a Germany tragically misunderstood without and often even within; of a Germany defeated again and again and thwarted in the fulfillment of her heroic mission in a blindly hostile world[9]. For them, the final linking with the Siegfried myth offered an ingenious device for the Cheruscan's ultimate apotheosis, for his rise—first to the status of a high-priest of all Germans and a victim of the gods, and then of a Teutonic superman and demigod.

* * * * *

Under the date of October 3, 1828, Eckermann records a conversation with Goethe concerning Fouqué's poetic efforts in the field of Germanic antiquity. "There is", Goethe remarked, "just as little to be gained for us from the somber (düster) Germanic antiquity as is the case with Serbian songs and similar barbarous poetry. One reads it and perhaps is interested for a time, but merely to outgrow it and leave it behind. Moreover, man's mind is sufficiently darkened by passions and the concept of fate without increasing the gloom through the obscurities of a primitive past. Man needs, most of all, clarity and serenity— — ."[10]

Thus spoke the sage of Weimar at the age of seventy-nine, who once in his youth had taken such genuine delight in simple poetry and folklore. However, the old Goethe's stern judgment also brings into focus the fact that the poetic treatment of certain topics from a primitive past must stand and fall with the symbolic meaning bestowed upon them by later generations. Once this inner relation to the new age ceases—once the myth-forming force of such legends subsides, their mission needs is ended. Then they wane and sink back to the level of mere historic facts or of antiquarian curiosities.

To this the story of the Arminius theme during the latter part of the nineteenth century—an age of progressive international rivalries, of liberalism, of national imperialism and socialism—forms no exception. It hardly could be otherwise. For this Arminius had long since developed into a symbol of heroic virtues and of truly unselfish leadership—into a symbol of courageous self-defense in the gigantic struggle for union and liberty in times of dire national extremity—very antipodes, indeed, to the spirit of aggressiveness latent in all modern power politics and national expansionism.

An age in which the principle of 'power for power's sake' triumphs—and power tends not only to corrupt but also to engender common fear and distrust which, in turn, breed hate—such an age will choose as its heroes men of a different mettle or else alter the qualities of the old heroes according to its own vision and standards.

Tacitus, to be sure, had endowed his Cheruscan fighter with ample tragic possibilities by implying Arminius' final fall from inner greatness through sheer lust of power. But later generations had brushed this fertile theme aside for propagandistic reasons. They purged their model warrior of such human failings, thus weakening, in the process, the stuff of which true human tragedy is made. They all but de-humanized their hero by making him an undeserved victim of lamentable human baseness—of unfounded suspicion and envy.

A morally strong opponent of the common political trends of the modern age—and there were many such conscientious dissenters in modern Germany too—could still have engraved Arminius' lofty name on novel standards by making him the prototype of great power used wisely—judiciously and benevolently—as Klopstock had attempted to do. Yet it hardly would have reflected the spirit dominant in the new age. Rather, it might have engendered another product of a dramatically feeble hero-worship after the Klopstock pattern.

The heroic culture-nation with a truly noble mission among the free peoples of this earth—a vision which once had inspired the exalted poet of the "Messiah"—did not, and hardly could have, come about. Instead of embracing a rôle of such moral leadership in a spirit of responsibility towards weaker and more backward peoples, this new Germany, now forcibly united, chose to drive forward along a path laid out before by her more powerful and more fortunate rivals abroad. As with them, enlightened political self-interest served her as her new banner. And, as a late-comer in the arena of such world-wide aspirations and activities, she rushed into the game with noiseful zest and vigor.

On the other hand, it can not be denied that the literary development of the Arminius theme quite strikingly reflects the protracted process of Germany's national coalescence as we follow the Cheruscan's rise and his subsequent metamorphosis from a mere tribal hero into a symbol of a heroic nation, of a culture-nation and, finally, of one united political entity. Social cohesion, with its roots in the family, works indeed in ever-widening circles. From family to tribe and nation, it gradually tends towards supra-national groups. With an ever-growing cultural exchange there also arises the challenge of an ideal world-communion: the 'One-World' dream of one common humanity living peaceably under the banner of 'equality and justice for all'. Beside the concept of one universal, secular empire—be it ancient Roman or Catholic medieval—there appears at once with early Christianity the dream of the sacred *civitas Dei*, with its mundane manifestation in a true *res publica Christiana*.

A strain of such idealistic tendency also underlies the unfolding of the Arminius theme as the defender of tribal independence gradually grows into the protagonist of German union and, ultimately, of common human freedom and justice. *There* lie the well-springs of its myth-forming force and the roots of its ideal grandeur.

Thus the emergence of the literary Arminius theme also reflects a growing awareness of the inner relation between the concept of human freedom and man's moral dependence and interdependence. But it also elucidates the contrast between true patriotism and its moral perversion, called nationalism which, in turn, might tend towards totalitarianism.

Moreover, the didactic quality of the best Arminius versions points at the undeniable truth that man's personal freedom can only be realized in a moral state; that the State and the concept of Liberty do not exclude but complement each other. Therefore Arminius has become, and is cherished as, the teacher of the manly *and* the moral virtues: of the devotion to one's nation and of the will to self-sacrifice in the hour of public peril. Arminius teaches that true freedom—the freedom inherent in all good citizenship—is at once an obligation and, as such, is far more precious than life itself. Arminius even calls for the training of good rulers: of princes and statesmen who reign—or serve— *within* the public and the moral law.

Conversely, the totalitarian state, in any of its ugly manifestations, is a case in point which proves what must happen when a primitive concept, like the *Führer-principle,* is superimposed upon a free, modern society: that it will sap its moral fiber; that it is bound to absorb the state and bring about the party-state and end in pagan state-idolatry. Such a state cannot but destroy man's freedom from within and return him to a condition of slavery which lurks behind all of its resounding promises and slogans.

It is indeed fortunate for the integrity of the ancient and venerable Arminius theme that no true modern poet of moral stature has ever attempted to debase it by turning Arminius, the guardian of man's most precious earthly good, Liberty, into a mere Hermann, the Aggressor and Suppressor.

APPENDIX*

PREFACE.

1. Ernst *Bickel*, in his 'Arminiusbiographie und Sagensigfried,' Bonn, 1949, renders an up-to-date account of the views of modern German historians about the historical Arminius figure.
2. Volume and scope of the scholarly investigations dealing with the poetical treatment of the Arminius theme are quite limited, indeed. There is as yet no comprehensive book on the enlightening subject. The existing researches are almost entirely in German and consist mainly of a few essays, extensive though partly obsolete, from the last quarter of the nineteenth century. To these must be added a few scholarly lectures of a more recent date which have appeared in print; as also a series of inaugural dissertations. The latter deal mainly with individual authors or with limited periods of the Arminius literature. The post-World-War-I period and the era of national socialism have engendered a considerable amount of new interest in the story of the heroic Cheruscan. However, the aims and results of both their poetic and scholarly productions on this subject have often to be viewed with an equal degree of caution.

The most up-to-date *bibliography* is offered by Wilhelm *Kosch* in the new edition of his *Literatur Lexikon*, January issue, 1950. It enumerates the poetic works dealing with Arminius and the Varus Battle (excluding the bulk of the shorter poems), as well as the scholarly researches.

Kurt *Bauerhorst*, in his Bibliographie der Stoff- und Motivgeschichte der deutschen Literatur, Berlin & Leipzig, 1932, p. 3, also presents a limited list of the main researches up to the time of his publication.

Wolfgang *Sydow*, in 'Deutung und Darstellung des Arminiusschicksals in seinen wesentlichen Ausprägungen,' Diss. Greifswald, 1937, offers a comprehensive list of 'Arminius Dichtungen' up to his own time—also minus the smaller poems—based mainly on the older edition of the Kosch Lexikon, of 1927-1930. Yet, both Kosch and Sydow omit those earlier poetical works in which Arminius plays but an incidental, though often most enlightening part, as with Frischlin, Moscherosch, and Rist. Both proceed directly from Hutten to Lohenstein and base their lists, at least up to about 1890, on the initial investigations by Riffert and von Wellenhof.

The few basic studies on the Arminius subject are:

W. *Creizenach*, 'Arminius in Poesie und Literaturgeschichte,' in Preussische Jahrbücher, Vol. 36, 1875, (not 1893, as stated by Bauerhorst).

Essay: brief introductory survey, apparently occasioned by the dedication of the Arminius Monument, near Detmold, in the same year.

J. E. *Riffert*, 'Die Hermannsschlacht in der deutschen Literatur,' in Herrigs Archiv für das Studium der neueren Sprachen und Literaturen, Vol. 63, 1880.

---

* Unless otherwise indicated, all translations into English, and all analyses of individual works, are the author's own.

Essay in serial publication. A comprehensive and thorough study of sources and motifs, up to the author's time.

P. von *Hofmann-Wellenhof*, 'Zur Geschichte des Arminius Cultus in der deutschen Literatur,' in Literarhistorische Abhandlungen, Grazer Schulprogramme, 1887/88.

Essays based upon, and supplementing, Riffert.

G. *Hauff*, 'Hermann und die Hermannsschlacht, hauptsächlich in der lyrischen Poesie des deutschen Volkes,' in Herrigs Archiv, Vol. 67, 1882.

Brief essay, supplementing Riffert's work in the field of lyrics.

L. *Jakobi*, 'Dramatische Behandlung des Arminiusstoffes von den Befreiungskriegen bis 1888,' Diss. Giessen, 1923.

W. *Sydow*, 'Deutung und Darstellung des Arminiusschicksals seit Kleist,' Diss. Griefswald, 1937.

K. *Holl*, 'Hermann und die Hermannsschlacht in der deutchen Dichtung.' Brief essay in *Festschrift* 'Hermann der Cherusker und sein Denkmal,' Detmold, 1925.

W. *Krogmann*, 'Das Arminiusmotiv in der deutschen Dichtung,' Wismar, 1933. A lecture.

Heinz *Kindermann*, 'Das Werden des Hermann-Mythus von Hutten bis Grabbe.'

Speech, printed in 'Kampf um die deutsche Lebensform,' Wien, 1940. (With Nazi bias.)

E. *Bickel*, 'Arminiusbiographie und Sagensigfried,' Bonn, 1949. (Cf. note 1 above.) Besides taking issue with the views of some modern historians concerning the historic Arminius figure, Bickel links Arminius to the Siegfried legend—still a topic of controversy.

More recent researches dealing with individual Arminius authors will be stated in the notes to those chapters.

3. cf. *Firiczek*, 'Arminiuslieder,' in Germanisch-Romanische Monatsschrift, 1914, p. 113, ff.

4. E. *Bickel*, (op. cit.) re-examines the classical sources quite cautiously in his study of Arminius' impact upon the course of Roman history and upon the decline of Roman imperialism. Then Bickel revives the theory of the identity of the historic Arminius figure with the Siegfried figure of the Nibelungen legend. "Arminius hat in der Siegfriedgestalt des germanisch-deutschen Mythus ein Fortleben bis zur Gegenwart gefunden" (p. 63).

According to Bickel, Arminius' aims were threefold: 1) Expulsion of Romans from Germany; 2) Alliance with, or conquest of, his rival, Marbod; 3) Unification of German tribes into a (defensive) federation—a premature and, hence, futile undertaking. Bickel neither recognizes a *'betrayal'* of the Romans on the part of the Roman 'officer,' Arminius, nor does he find any cause for a *tragic conflict within the hero* over his *double allegiance* to Rome *and* his people. For Bickel claims to prove from the Latin sources that the Cheruscan had never been anything but the leader of a temporary auxiliary contingent *voluntarily* operating with the Roman legions in Germany. As such, Bickel asserts, Arminius was free to leave the Roman army of Tiberius when his assistance was no longer needed (6 A.D.) Arminius even may never have been in Rome, Bickel holds. The Cheruscan had learned his Latin—and Roman strategy—in camps and on campaigns, where, for several years, he was the close companion of Velleius. The memory of his *German* name—which may have been *Siguard* (then changed to Sigurd and Sigfried)—has been lost. From the Romans he received citizenship and 'knighthood' for his valorous deeds—an honor which Arminius shared with other German nobles—by being adopted into the Etruscan-Roman *gens Arminia*; hence his Roman name. His brother Flavius, however, became and always remained an officer and partisan of Rome while Arminius, upon his return home, joined, strengthened, and reorganized the faction of the anti-Roman 'patriots.' Bickel's main reasons for linking the fate of Arminius once more with that of the legendary Siegfried are as follows:

1) Proceeding from the Germanic name Siguard (the stem Sig- being customary in Arminius' family), Bickel stresses the striking similarity of the final fate of both heroes—both are *jugendliche Lichtgestalten* and fall victim to a scheming kin, their in-laws.

2) Siegfried comes from *Xanten* (ad Sanctos; now Birten), the former *Castra Vetera* of the Roman legions, whither the remnants of Varus' decimated army fled, and whence the Roman campaigns into northern Germany proceeded: 'central seat of all knowledge of ancient Germany.' In short, when, during the centuries of migrations and early Christianization, the memory of the historical Cheruscan hero grew dim, it lived on as an *oral* and *local tradition* in the vicinity of Xanten in order to rise anew, centuries later, in the disguise of the Siegfried myth.

Bickel is a historian and takes issue with his predecessors in the study of the historic Arminius, from *Mommsen* (Römische Geschichte, Vol. V, p. 6), who had interpreted Arminius "from the Roman standpoint," i.e., understating the hero's qualities and historical significance—to *Hohl's* 'Zur Lebensgeschichte des Siegers im Teutoburger Walde,' in Historische Zeitschrift, # 167, 1943, pp. 457 ff.; and *Hohl's* 'Neues von Arminius,' in *Zeitschrift* Die alten Sprachen, 1943, pp. 49 ff.

Bickel's final goal is "to place the historical portrait of Arminius beside the poetical interpretations" (p. 13), thus helping to refute the distorted picture of the 'ideal German' of the past as established by recent national socialist interpreters. Moreover, Bickel places Arminius in a direct line with Vercingetorix, the Celt, and with Hannibal, as the three great enemies of expansive Roman imperialism. Only Arminius succeeded where the other two failed; though the Cheruscan remained unsuccessful in his second major aim: German unification—*a defensive union, not conquest.*

5. cf. Wilhelm *Kosch*, op. cit., and Wolfgang *Sydow*, op. cit., Appendix. No bibliography of the poetic interpretations of the Arminius theme can possibly claim completeness. None states the references to and the descriptions of Arminius and the Varus Battle in medieval chronicles. Some do not even mention those works where the hero appears but incidentally. No list comprises all the poems which deal with, or just mention, the fate of Arminius (Hermann) himself, or that of the members of his family. The same holds true for the mention of the Varus Battle.

The works listed by Kosch and Sydow can be grouped in the following categories:
Poetic 'Arminius publications' between *Hutten's* famous Dialogue and *Grabbe's* drama: about 49; between *Grabbe* and the year *1938*, about 83; an approximate total of titles known and listed: 132.
If, for some pertinent reasons, we do divide the time between Hutten (1520) and World War II (about 415 years) into two periods:
1) from Hutten to Grabbe, or 315 years, and
2) from Grabbe to World War II, or 100 years, we arrive at the following picture:
Period I is represented with approximately 29 dramas, 3 operas and 'Singspiele,' 4 epics or lengthy heroic poems; 9 smaller poems (such as odes, etc.); 1 prose tale; and 2 Arminius versions of an undefined poetic form (lit. form not stated; only titles given).
Period II, on the other hand, comprising less than one third of the former in duration of time, offers 53 dramas, 3 operas, 9 epics, 4 larger poems, 5 prose tales, 4 novels, 1 or 2 modern radio adaptations ('Funkspiele'), plus 3 unidentified literary specimens.
Thus the last one century offers almost double the amount of Arminius versions over the previous three centuries combined. The dramatic form prevails throughout: 53 for the last one hundred years, as against 29 of the earlier period. Operas stand 3 : 3; epics and larger poems about 9 : 4, in favor of the last century; smaller poems 9 : 4, in favor of Period I (so far as titles are obtainable). Poetic prose tales 1 : 9, in favor of Period II. The first attempt at a rendition of our theme in novel form originated in 1862. The remaining novels, characteristically enough, represent the most recent interpretations of Arminius, mostly from the pen of enthusiastic supporters of the new *Bewegung*. They often celebrate the ancient Cheruscan as the father of the *'Führerprinciple,'* as the awakener of racial self-consciousness, and as the first one to envision the federative principle among the early Germans—the first prematurely to strive and tragically to die for it.

6. Foremost among them the dramatists Otto Ludwig and Gerhart Hauptmann.

INTRODUCTION.

1. Mâze: the ideal of chivalry in deportment and actions; mastery of self.
2. The legend was first attached to Frederick II, last great emperor of the Hohenstaufen dynasty, and later transferred to the more popular Frederick I, called Barbarossa.
3. Appropriately referred to in English as the Germanies.
4. cf. Lohenstein's Arminius later.
5. Enea Silvio in his geographic treatise *Europa*.
6. Irenikus, *Germaniae exegesis*, 8 vols., 1517/18.
7. Heinrich Bebel, *Proverbia Germanica*, 1508.
8. Jordanus, *De praerogativa Romani imperii*, about 1280.
9. Aventinus, Three Books of German History, in Latin, 1531.
10. cf. Lohenstein's 'Arminius' again.
11. 1520.

12. cf. Moscherosch and Rist later.
13. cf. F. K. Moser, *Vom deutschen Nationalgeist*, 1765. Though Moser advocates a warm national patriotism, he rejects the militant, enlightened absolutism of Berlin, its Spartan spirit, as did many other patriots of that age.
14. cf. Schlegel, Moeser, and many others.
15. in 1748 ff.
16. 'The education of mankind'—a favorite topic with the enlightened German classicists.
17. The Bismarck and the Hitler eras.

CHAPTER I.

Literature:

1. Karl Brandi, *Deutsche Geschichte*, Berlin, 1919, p. 7.
2. Richard Reitzenstein, *Tacitus und sein Werk*, in 'Neue Wege zur Antike,' IV, 1926.
3. Moritz Schuster, *Römische Literaturgeschichte*, in Walzel's 'Handbuch der Literaturwissenschaft'.

Notes:

4. Annals II, 88.
5. Roman History, P. II, 117/18.
6. cf. E. Bickel, op. cit., chapter I.
7. ibid., chapter III.
8. Hagen in 'The Lay of the Nibelungs'.
9. op. cit. II, 118: ardorem animi vultu oculisque praeferens.
10. op. cit. II, 63.
11. op. cit. II, 88.
12. op. cit. II, 117: (Syria)—quam pauper divitem ingressus dives pauperem reliquit.
13. ibid.
14. Annals, I, 57.
15. ibid.., quoted from the Thomas Gordon translation. We recall the monumental Roman presentation of Thusnelda being led in chains before the triumphal chariot of the Roman victor.
16. Annals, I, 60.
17. ibid. II, 44.
18. ibid. 88; quoted from Gordon's translation.
20. ibid.

CHAPTER II.

Literature.

Paul Joachimsen, *Tacitus im deutschen Humanismus*, in 'Neue Jahrbücher für das deutsche Altertum,' # 27.
Ludwig Geiger, *Renaissance und Humanismus in Italien und Deutschland*, Berlin, 1882.
Ulrich von Hutten, *Gespräche*, transl. and edit. by David Frdr. Strauss, Leipzig, 1860.
David Frdr. Strauss, *Ulrich von Hutten*, Leipzig 1895.

Notes.
1. Tacitus, *Annals* II, 88.
2. Paul Joachimsen, op. cit., p. 697 ff.
3. Ludwig Geiger, op. cit., p. 333 ff
4. 1517.
5. 1520.
6. cf. *Annals* II, 88.
7. ibid. I and II.
8. Roman History, II, 117/18.
9. Transl. into German as 'Totengespräch,' publ. in 1507.
10. Arminius' similarity to Siegfried has often been emphasized; cf. Bickel.
11. This seems to be Hutten's own addition, though it could have been suggested by Tacitus' introduction to his *Agricola* where Tacitus compares the danger of the East with that of the North, the German.
12. *Arminius*, # 41.
13. ibid. # 43.

CHAPTER III.
Notes.
1. Wimpheling, *Epitoma rerum Germanicarum*, 1505, Vol. I, 706.
2. Aventinus, *Chronika*, I, 28. The work originated between 1526 and 1533 and was published in 1566. The Latin version, *'Annals,'* appeared in Ingolstadt, in 1554.
3. Notice *German* prince—no longer tribal Cheruscan.
4. There are over 400 Luther letters addressed to Spalatin preserved from the years 1519 to 1521 alone. Luther affectionately called Spalatin 'old Pylades.'
5. Transl. by Simon Schardius in Historicum opus I, pp. 257-298; also reprinted in the excellent source book *Schardius Redivivus*, or Rerum Germanicarum scriptores varii, Giessen, 1673.
6. cf. J. E. Riffert, op. cit., p. 162 ff.
7. cf. such revealing titles as Erpoldus Lindenbruch's *Chronica of the Praiseworthy* (löblichen) *Hero Arminius* (in German), 1589; and Matthias Quad von Kinkelbach's *The Glory* (Herrlichkeit) *of the German Nation*, Cologne, 1609.
8. In Rochus W. von Liliencron, *Die historischen Volkslieder der Deut'schen vom 13. zum 16. Jahrhundert*, Vol. IV, 460 ff; also quoted in part, and briefly discussed, by Riffert, op. cit.
9. Let us abide by Thy word, Put an end to the Pope's and the Spaniards' bloodshed.
10. Liliencron, op. cit., Vol. IV, p. 302.
11. 'Gesichte,' P. II, # 1, 1642.
12. The name must be an allusion to the family name of Aventinus, who is quoted repeatedly in the course of the trial.
13. Moscherosch knew de Quevedo in the French version, *Les Visions de Don Francesco*, Caen, 1633.
14. Aventinus, Book IV, p. 189.
15. Grimmelshausen's *Simplicissimus*, 1668.
16. Allegorical plays with predominantly religious musical interludes.

CHAPTER IV.

Literature:
1. Wilhelm Scherer, *Deutsche Literaturgeschichte*, 1883, (p. 379).
2. Wilhelm Dilthey, *Analyse des Menschen seit Renaissance und Reformation*, in 'Gesammelte Schriften,' Vol. II.
3. Luise Laporte, *Lohensteins Arminius*, in Germanische Studien, # 48, Berlin 1927.

Notes:
4. op. cit., p. 251 ff.
5. cf. Tacitus' *Annals*, II, 88.
6. Lohenstein actually anticipates some of the basic Nazi claims by 250 years: elect individuals, and an elect class, among the elect people (nation). cf. also such arrogant titles of recent books as Jörg Lechler's *Five Thousand Years of Germany*, Leipzig, 1936, with its inner similarity to Lohenstein's *'Urnation.'*
7. First edition of Lohenstein's *Arminius* appeared in Leipzig, in 1689. Present quotation from the Introduction to 2nd. edition, of 1731, p. LII.
8. ibid. p. LXXXVII.
9. ibid.
10. Hamlet III, 2.
11. cf. the motto to Wieland's novel *Agathon*: Quid virtus et quid sapientia possit, Utile nobis proposuit exemplum.
12. The humanists' antithesis of the 'vita activa' and the 'vita contemplativa' reappears here, though ethically deepened.
13. cf. Lohenstein's *Arminius* II, p. 218-220; II, 410, and many other passages. Compare Leibniz' principle of the 'pre-established harmony,' cosmic counterpart to all sacred political and social absolutism of the Age of Reason.
14. Lohenstein's *Arminius* I, 138.
15. The 2nd edition is divided into four parts, with four or five books each.
16. There are two sons of Arminius and Thusnelda in this novel and both are born in Germany; one is 'baptized' in the Rhine.
17. Tacitus' *Annals* II, 88: Adgandester's plot and the Romans.
18. Henry C. Lancaster, *History of French Dramatic Literature in the 17th Century*, P. IV, Vol. I, p. 247 f., (1929).
19. Riffert, op. cit., p. 263.
20. The noted musicologist, Alfred Einstein, informs me that Johann Adolf Scheibe's (not Scheiten, as Riffert has it), libretto was never set to music. According to Prof. Einstein, this libretto was formerly at the Königl. Bibliothek in Berlin. The Hasse(n) libretto was formerly available at the libraries in Dresden, Munich and Wolfenbüttel, as also at the Conservatories of Naples and Milan. The Salvi libretto, according to Einstein, was also set to music by Händel; cf. 'Werke,' Vol. 39.
21. published posthumously, in 1725.

CHAPTER V.

Literature.

Johann Elias Schlegel, *Werke*, Vols. 1 and 5, Berlin & Kopenhagen, 1770.
J. Rentsch, *Elias Schlegel als Trauerspieldichter*, Diss. Erlangen, 1890.
Eugen Wolff, *Joh. Elias Schlegel*, Berlin 1889.
Justus Möser, *Arminius, Ein Trauerspiel*, Braunschweig, 1749.
Walter A. Montag, Kornelius von Ayrenhoffs Verdienste um das Wiener Theater, Diss. Münster, 1908.
Max Stückmann, *Klopstocks Bestrebungen um die Begründung eines neuen deutschen Volkstums*, Diss. Greifswald, 1924.
A. Redeker, *Klopstock und der deutsche Staat*, Diss. München, 1930.
Karl-Heinz Kröplin, *Klopstocks Hermannsdrama*, Diss. Rostock, 1934.
Franz Muncker, *Klopstock*, Berlin 1900.
ed. Franz Muncker, Christ. Martin Wieland, *Hermann*; in Deutsche Literaturdenkmale des 18. ten Jahrhunderts, # 6, 1882.

Notes:

1. *Hecuba*, 1736. Its later, revised version bears the title of *The Trojan Women*.
2. In Gottsched's 'Deutsche Schaubühne,' P. IV, 1743.
3. Muncker, op. cit., p. 390.
4.   Cling to the land, the dear land of thy sires,
       Grapple to that with thy whole heart and soul!
       Thy power is rooted deep and strongly here.
       But in yon' stranger world thou'lt stand alone,
       A trembling reed beat down by every blast.   (II, 1.)
   (Transl. by Sir Theodore Martin, in Harvard Classics, Vol. 26.)
5. I, 2.
6. Reprinted in 'Deutsche Schaubühne zu Wien,' P. II, Wien 1762.
7. B. R. Abeken, Berlin, 1843.
8. Works, Vol. 9, p. 201 ff.
9. op. cit., p. 274.
10. Only the first edition of this work has been available to me. The 2nd, of 1753, which shows Gottsched's revisions, was out of reach.
11. Letter of April 4, 1753.
12. cf. Ayrenhoff's 'Autobiography,' of 1804, which reveals him as a harbinger of the later '*gross-deutsch*' movement. Both he and Möser think in terms of nations, not of petty dynasties and states.
13. *Hermanns Tod*, III, In the last Roman's blood I aim to strike down tyranny. Revenge, justice and happiness I seek for all mankind.
14. Letters to Gleim, of Dec. 1758 and Febr. 1759.
15. cf. Schiller later.
16. cf. Walter A. Montag, op. cit.
17. op. cit., p. 285.
18. For discord is Germany's worst enemy.
19. The Muncker edition mentioned above. Exact date of the completion of the manuscript seems to be in doubt.
20. op. cit.
21. P. von Hofmann-Wellenhof, op. cit., P. III, p. 11.

22. Sing, oh immortal Muse, the redemption of sinful Man.
23. I ponder the noble and awesome thought of being worthy of thee, my Fatherland.
24. cf. Alfred Redeker, op. cit.; also Fr. Muncker, op. cit., and Heinz Kindermann, Klopstocks Entdeckung der Nation, Danzig, 1935, (the latter with Nazi bias).
25. The bard's instrument.
26. The Franks to France; the Anglo-Saxons to England.
27. Never was there a nation fairer towards others.
    Do not be too fair; they are not noble enough
    To see how noble your weakness is.
28. Your ways are modest and wise.
    Your spirit is earnest and deep,
    Yet you gladly forge your sword
    Into the plough. Hail to Thee! It is not
    Defiled by the blood of foreign nations.
29. —but then they drew their swords against him;
    And in his blood lies he whose soul embraced
    The noble thought of Fatherland.
30. Letter of Dec. 31, 1768.
31. You are like the strongest, shadiest oak
    In the innermost grove,
    Like the highest, oldest, most sacred oak,
    Oh Fatherland!
32. The ode *Hermann und Thusnelda*.
33. Many of these names stem from Lohenstein's *Arminius*.
34. cf. Tacitus' motif of the meeting of the hostile brothers before the battle of Idistavisus.

CHAPTER VI.

For the time between the publication of Klopstock's first *bardiet*, *Hermannsschlacht* (1767), and the origin of Kleist's drama of the same name (1808), 11 Arminius versions have been recorded. They consist of 7 plays, two by Ayrenhoff, 1768 and 1774; Casparson, 1771; Reichsiegel, 1777; Bodmer, 1778; Fresenius, 1784, and August Schumann, 1795. There are also 1 ode by Cramer, 1774; 1 bardic song by Kretschmann, 1769; 1 heroic poem by von Babo, 1779/80; and 1 Arminius version, unidentified as to literary form, by Oberleiter, 1782. Patzke's libretto to a 'Singspiel,' of 1780, should be mentioned, too. However, Klopstock's own odes and his other two *bardiete* are not included in this list.

For the interval between Grabbe's drama (1836) and the Ludwig fragment (1851) we find 5 plays, 2 epic poems, and one heroic poem recorded. The only name of any distinction among these authors is that of the eminent scholar, Hermann Grimm, son of Wilhelm Grimm, whose insignificant Arminius drama appeared in the year of Otto Ludwig's fragment, 1851.

For the period after Otto Ludwig, reference to the lists by Kosch and Sydow (op. cit.), may suffice.

Literature.

Kleist, *Werke*, 5 vols., edit. Erich Schmidt, Bibliogr. Inst., Leipzig, 1904/05.
Heinrich Meyer-Benfey, *Die Dramen Heinrich von Kleists*, Göttingen, 1911.
Otto Fraude, *Kleists Hermannschlacht auf der Bühne*, Kiel, 1919.
Walter Silz, *Heinrich von Kleist's Conception of the Tragic*, Baltimore, 1923.
Walter Silz, *Early German Romanticism. Its Founders and Heinrich von Kleist*, Cambridge, 1929.
Georg Hempel, *Heinrich von Kleists Hermannsschlacht*, Diss. Erlangen, 1931.
Erich Hagemeister, *Fouqué als Dramatiker*, Diss. Greifswald, 1905.
Chr. D. Grabbe, *Werke*, ed. Wukadinowic, Berlin, 1905.
Eduard Duller, *Grabbes Leben*, Düsseldorf, 1838.
Otto Nieten, *Grabbe, sein Leben und seine Werke*, Dortmund, 1908.
A. Kutscher, *Hebbel und Grabbe*, München, 1913.
F. J. Schneider, *Christ. D. Grabbe*, München, 1934.
Otto Ludwig, *Werke*, ed. Viktor Schweitzer, Bibliogr. Inst., Leipzig, 1898.
Moritz Heydrich, *Skizzen und Fragmente*, Leipzig, 1874.
Heinrich Kraeger, *Entwürfe Otto Ludwigs zu einem Hermanndrama*, Berlin, 1930, in 'Germanische Studien,' # 79.
Paul Schlenther, *Gerhart Hauptmann*, Berlin, 1912.
Hans von Hülsen, *Gerhart Hauptmann*, Berlin, 1932.
Paul Fechter, *Gerhart Hauptmann*, Dresden, 1934.

Notes.

1. Walter Silz, *Early German Romanticism* (op. cit.), p. 86.
2. The Spanish people's revolt against Napoleon of 1809.
3. Unworthy is the nation
   That does not gladly stake its all
   Upon its honor.
4. There is a limit to the despot's power!
5. A band of brothers true we swear to be,
   Never to part in danger or in death.
   (From the Martin transl.)
6. Be one, be one, be one!
7. The strong man is still strongest when alone.
8. Murder him (Napoleon)! Judgment Day will not ask you for your reasons!
9. What! Let them try, forsooth, to force on us
   A yoke we are determined not to bear!
10. In such a struggle I must stand alone.
11. Old Germanic prophetess.
12. Woe to thee, my Fatherland! To sing thy glory Is denied to me, thy loyal bard!
13. Walter Silz, *Early German Romanticism* (Op. cit.), p. 75 ff.
14. ibid.
15. cf. F. J. Schneider, op. cit., p. 320.
16. Letter to Ambrunn of April 15, 1851.
17. Letter to Ambrunn of Dec. 25, 1851.
18. The 'Jungdeutsch' movement.

19. Am grossen Werke müssen viele wirken.
20. Der Feige lebt—doch nur dem Edlen folgt
    Der Ruhm—
21. Annotation from notebook II: Ein Stoff für alle; eine Form für viele; ein Gehalt für die Besten.

CONCLUSION.

1. cf. Adolf Römheld, *Die Varusschlacht*, Drama, Leipzig, 1915. Römheld also uses the Siegfried motif, as well as Grabbe's *Schollengebundenheit*—the rooting of the hero in his home soil. The author shares with Grabbe many of the latter's absurdities.
2. cf. The titles and sub-titles of the following novels of the period:
   H. Heyk, *Arminius der Cherusker, Ein deutscher* Roman, Leipzig, 1932 & 1925.
   Hjalmar Kutzleb, *Der erste Deutsche, Roman Hermanns des Cheruskers*, Braunschweig, Berlin & Hamburg, 1934 & '36.
   Paul Albrecht, *Arminius Sigurfried, Ein Roman des deutschen Volkes*, Berlin, 1935.
   Albrecht even attempts a complete fusion of the Arminius theme with the Siegfried myth.
   Hildegard Wiegand, *Arminius, Ein Siegfriedschicksal*, Leipzig, Strassburg, Zürich, 1934 and 1935.
   The daemonic hero of this widely-read novel strives to unite all Germans in 'one realm of *this* world.'
3. Sydow, op. cit., p. 22.
4. The basic problems of these Arminius versions are:
   1) the personal relationship between leader and retinue, *Führer und Volk*.
   2) Submission to leadership, and personal liberty.
5. According to Sydow, p. 20, Arminius is the first German to fight, and tragically to die for, these problems.
   cf. also B. Marckwardt in *Geschichte der deutschen Poetik*, Introd. to Vol. I, Berlin, 1937.
6. Yet Sydow also demands of the poet *Ehrfurcht vor der Geschichte*—respect for historical truth.
7. First adapted for open-air performance by Iltz and Bacmeister, then repeatedly performed on the stage since 1934. Grabbe's satire was hailed by the press of those days as 'the most German of all German plays.'
8. The term '*völkisch*' is difficult to render in English. In addition to the meaning of 'national,' it carries a definite 'racial' connotation. Moreover, the '*Volk*' is sacred and always good, whereas its princes, or *Führer*, may be bad.
9. cf. the influential Nazi writer A. Möller van den Bruck and his Arminius essay in vol. 7 of his book *Die Deutschen*. Möller calls Arminius the 'central figure in the initial history of our race.'
10. Johann Peter Eckermann, *Gespräche mit Goethe*, Vol. I, 1823-1827.
    "Es ist in der altdeutschen Zeit," sagte Goethe, "ebenso wenig für uns zu holen, als wir aus den serbischen Liedern und ähnlichen bar-

barischen Volkspoesien gewonnen haben. Man liest und interessiert sich wohl eine Zeit lang dafür, aber bloss um es abzutun und sodann hinter sich zu lassen. Der Mensch wird überhaupt genug durch seine Leidenschaften und Schicksale verdüstert, als dass er nötig hätte, dieses noch durch die Dunkelheiten einer barbarischen Vorzeit zu tun. Er bedarf der Klarheit und Aufheiterung—"

www.ingramcontent.com/pod-product-compliance
Lightning Source LLC
Chambersburg PA
CBHW031315150426
43191CB00005B/245